CONTROLLING YOUR

DAILY DEMONS

CONTROLLING YOUR

DAILY DEMONS

Rev. Matt Harper

iUniverse, Inc.
New York   Bloomington

Controlling Your Daily Demons

iUniverse books may be ordered through booksellers or by contacting:

iUniverse
1663 Liberty Drive
Bloomington, IN 47403
www.iuniverse.com
1-800-Authors (1-800-288-4677)

ISBN: 978-1-4401-1067-2 (pbk)
ISBN: 978-1-4401-1066-5 (ebk)

Printed in the United States of America

iUniverse rev. date: 1/5/2009

Contents

ACKNOWLEDGEMENTS

To my family: Mrs. Deborah Harper, my daughter Dr. D. Devonne Harper and my son Mr. J. Gordon Harper for their encouragement and editorial assistance

To my senior pastors Reverends Kenneth and Cassandra Marcus of

Turner Chapel AMEC Marietta, GA for providing inspiration, spiritual growth and facility to teach and develop some of the messages in this work

To Reverend Ricardo Privette and family of Durham NC; thank you, my good friend and brother in Christ for your encouragement and editorial assistance.

ABOUT THE AUTHOR

A hopeless sinner heated in the fiery furnaces of life and molded to serve GOD.

Preface

Basic Premise of book: Each of us is tempted many times each day to do things we know are wrong. We must resist these temptations if we are to have any order in our lives and if our civilization is to survey.

You knew it was wrong and can't understand why you did it. What drives us to do these wrong things? Why are we sometimes so out of control? Have you ever asked yourself these questions? Most of us have, perhaps on a daily basis.

The Bible attributes our doing the wrong thing when we really want to do what is right to the influences of sin spirits upon our lives. *Now if I do what I do not want to do, it is no longer I who do it, but it is sin (sinful spirits) living in me that does it. Ro. 7:20 NIV.* . I call these sinful spirits **Daily Demons.**

These Daily Demons are Satan's little helpers who try to influence our decisions by continually sowing various sinful **Daily Temptations** in our lives. The goal of this book is to make readers more keenly aware of these sinful influences that attacks and tempts them every day.

We need to be aware of these influences and we must also understand how to resist and keep them under control. Problem is sin is very sneaky. It enters your life a little at a time and before you realize it you are surrounded by it. The danger in being around sin is you become accustomed to it. Once you become acclimated to sin you then begin to assimilate sinful acts. Here are a few example to illustrate how easily and subtly sin can slip into our lives.

Your clock alarms and you push the snooze button for an extra ten minutes of sleep. You do this twice and now you are behind schedule. Traffic is heavy and you are falling more behind. You know your boss will be furious if you are late again this week. The traffic light changes from red to green and the driver talking on the cell phone in front of you doesn't see the change. You honk your horn and the driver flips you the bird. Your temper flares and you want to ram the rear of his car. The Daily Demons are at work sowing Daily Temptations in your path.

A former worker at your firm left behind a finished report on your desk without a signature. You give the report to your boss who reads it and, mistakenly, gives you high praise for doing an excellent job. You know this could lead to bigger things for your career. You also know that taking credit for someone else's work is wrong and against company policy. What would you do? The Daily Demons are sowing Daily Temptations in your path.

Six weeks ago you promised your family you would take them on a camping trip this weekend. However, you just got invited to fill a vacant spot in a foursome this weekend at the best golf club in the city. You consider lying to your family telling them you have to work over the weekend. The Daily Demons are sowing Daily Temptations in your path.

You are walking behind an elderly lady in the parking lot when she removes her car keys from her purse dropping an object on the pavement. As you approach the object you see it is a small wad of cash. You have ample time to call the lady before she leaves. However, you are currently unemployed and desperately need this cash.

The Daily Demons are at work sowing Daily Temptations in your path.

You moved into a new neighborhood and a new neighbor gave you a very expensive bottle of wine as a welcome gift not knowing you are a recovering alcoholic. The Daily Demons are at work sowing Daily Temptations in your path.

We all face a seemingly endless number of temptations everyday and we have little or no control of this. However, we can control what we think, say, and do in response to these temptations. These are the critical parts of our lives, thoughts, words and deeds.

Regardless of your religious beliefs or lack thereof, we all sometimes take actions we know or feel are morally and or legally wrong. How we feel after doing these wrong actions is what divides us into two broad groups; Christians who are saved and believe in and accept Jesus as their Lord and Savior, and those who are not saved.

As Christians we know we are sinful by nature and only God's grace keeps us from falling into the clutches of all manner of sinful living. Satan knows we all have a sinful nature; after all he planted the seed of sin in us through Adam long ago. The good news is as Christians we have a far more powerful force at work in us, the Holy Spirit. Let me assure you our Holy Spirit can and will defeat any Daily Temptations that come against us; *and God is faithful, he will not let you be tempted beyond what you can bear. But when you are tempted, he will also provide a way out so that you can stand up under it. I Co. 10:13 NIV.*

For most of us our lives we are divided into three zones each containing a myriad of temptations. Our **personal zone** is where we are involved with inner-self generated emotions. These are things that influence our behavior based on who we are inside without any external stimuli. Our **family zone** is where we interact with family members and perhaps close friends.

Our actions in these relationships are very critical because these relationships are close, long lasting and can continue to impact our lives and the lives of our friends and family members for a long time. Our **social zone** includes work associates, neighbors and the general public. There are no boundaries for Daily Temptations, they can and do appear in any zone, area or time of one's life.

A MORNING PRAYER

GOD I thank you for awaking me this morning with a
sound mind and a healthy body.

Thank you Lord for being with me and guiding me
safely through yet another night.

Thank you Lord for each blessing, all your mercies and
all your grace.

Lord I pray that as I go through this day the words

of my mouth and the meditations of my heart

will be acceptable in your sight.

Lord I pray that your Holy Spirit in me will guide

me so that my every thought, word and deed

will be in accordance with your will and

your purpose.

Lord I pray that everything I do and everything I say

this day will be a living witness and a living testimony to

someone who is lost in the world so that they may

come to you accepting your salvation and live

Christian lives serving you.

Amen.

WHY THESE FORCES
INFLUENCE OUR DECISIONS

But each one is tempted when, by his own

evil desire, he is dragged away and enticed.

Then, after desire has conceived, it gives

birth to sin; and sin, when it is full-grown,

gives birth to death. James 1:14-15. NIV.

James made it very clear; we yield to temptations in our lives because of our own evil desires for worldly things. A Journey to Christian Maturity represents the steps in a person's life as they grow in Christ becoming more capable of resisting the evil desires of their flesh. There is a circled **U** at the left side of the chart followed by a circled **S** and a circled **H**.

The **U** is for **UNSAVED** the **S** is for SAVED and the **H** is for **HOLINESS**. One line segment connects the U and S circles and another connects the S and H circles. The segment connecting U and S circles represent the unsaved portion of a person's life while the other, connecting the S and H circles, represents the saved or Christian portion of a person's life.

Each line segment is surrounded by sin circles (Note: sin presents it self in all shapes, forms and sizes, not just circles) representing the various sins that tempt us daily. When an arrow points to a sin circles it indicates the person has yielded to the temptation of that sin circle by indulging in that sin. Notice during the unsaved portion of this person's life he/she yielded to every sin that tempted him/her.

That is a very uninhibited and sinful person. However, most people that have not accepted Christ do have some limits as to what sins they will or will not commit. Let's take a very simplistic look at how the DTs try to influence our daily activities.

You are diabetic and must avoid sweets. However, today is Sunday and you tell yourself another piece of carrot cake won't increase my glucose level very much. An inner-voice, reminds you this is the wrong thing to do. So begins another personal decision conflict. This is seemingly a very simple decision. However, it is a very real test of your will. Will you yield to the temptation to satisfy the flesh and eat the cake or will you do what is right to protect your God given body and resist the temptation?

It is at this point the little Daily Demons come into play. Just as the Holy Spirit is with us at all times, the Daily Demons are always on the job and they arrive with a briefcase full of Daily Temptations. This simple example of resisting carrot cake shows how the Daily Demons and Daily Temptations work.

First the Daily Demons know you have a fondness for carrot cake because it's their job to know all your weaknesses, so they present this Daily Temptation (the cake) and encourage you to eat to excess which is both sinful and unhealthy. When you resist the temptation they attack you with plan B which is to help you rationalize why eating too much carrot cake is justified.

Problem is, the Daily Demons don't really help you rationalize, but they do help you **RATIONAL-LIES**, which is to develop RATIONAL-LIES to justify your wrong actions. Rational-lies are illogical reasons we use to justify doing something we should not do. In this case the rational-lie may be I will have a diet drink with the carrot cake and that will balance everything out, keep me healthy and prevent me from gaining weight. In other words, they help you lie to yourself and believe it.

Daily Demons are Satan's disciples; they work for him. Their job is to tempt people into doing things that are against God's will, one of the least of which is eating carrot cake in an excessive amount.

People who don't believe in God have little or no conflict with temptations; they just follow their feeling and or emotions. If it feels good and /or there is material gain to be had they will indulge the temptation. They will use phrases such as you only live once, the strongest survives, all is fair in love and war, It is only business, the ends always justifies the means, and God knows my heart etc. to justify (and/or **rational-lies**) their sinful acts.

These sinful forces are at work in us because we were, by the transgression of Adam and Eve, born with a sinful nature which leads us to pursue evil desires. However; the good new is, just like Adam and Eve, we have a choice. Therefore, we can yield to sin or we can resist it and follow God. *"God will not let you be tempted beyond what you can bear; He will provide a way out of your temptations"* I Corinth. 10:13.

Our physical senses: feel, sight, smell, hear, and taste, are pathways that daily temptations use to enter our lives. We see our neighbors with a new car and the process begins. Will we be happy for our neighbor or will envy creep into our thoughts? How we respond to our

Daily Temptations is determined by our level of Christian maturity. If we are strong Christians we will rejoice with our neighbors in celebrating their gifts from God while continuing to thank God for our blessings.

People accepting Christ is an act that greatly angers Satan because this means he has just lost one of his disciples. Therefore Satan will begin to use all his power to win the new Christian back to his team. Satan will place many temptations in the path of the new Christian and he will try the new Christian in every area of weakness.

This is why Christians must maintain a strong knowledge of God's Word, develop and maintain a working relationship with God, and keep close fellowship with other Christians. That way they are empowered to resist Satan's relentless temptations. Consider engineers, doctors, plumbers and even criminals; they all have meetings where they share ideas, grow from each other's experiences and support each other. This is a fellowship. Likewise, Christians should fellowship in Sunday school, bible studies and other Christian activities in order to grow, to support each other and become stronger Christians.

A mistake many new and not so new Christians make is to think they will become perfect after accepting Christ. They wrongly think they will some how become immune to sin. Nothing could be further from the truth. Sin is in all of us and we will never be immune to it. Let me use an analogy to illustrate my point.

Imagine a large sponge that has been used to clean-up a dirty greasy mess on a kitchen floor. The sponge is totally saturated with dirt, grime and filth. If the sponge is not cleaned germs will multiply and it will begin to rot and deteriorate until it is destroyed. You look at this sponge and see that it is a good sponge and that it could be used for your purpose.

So you begin to clean the sponge by washing it in detergent. Each time you repeat the cleaning process the sponge becomes cleaner but there is still some filth in the sponge. Try as you may you can not get all the dirt out of the sponge.

If you apply enough pressure some dirt will still come from the sponge. However, you realize the sponge is clean enough to be used for your purpose. Sinners are like the sponge; Satan has dragged them through the dirt filth and evils of the world until they are completely saturated with sin and **Satan wants the sinners to deteriorate and die**.

Then God comes along and chooses the sinner as one of his own. God begins the process of cleaning the sinner and after each trial (cleaning cycle) the sinner grows stronger in his walk with Christ. Each trial the sinner faces will make him stronger and cleaner until God decides the sinner is ready to do his work.

There will always be some sin (dirt) in a Christian's life but he is **acceptable to God**. Our walk with God will lead us to a more holy life, but not perfection. Only God is perfect and we must remember this and not get discouraged when we yield to temptations. We must repent for our sins, pray to God for forgiveness and the strength to resist temptation, and continue on our Christian journey to holiness.

WHY DO WE HAVE TRIALS IN OUR LIVES?

Consider it pure joy, my brothers, whenever

you face trials of many kinds, because

you that the testing of your faith develops

perseverance. Perseverance must finish it's

work so that you may be mature and complete,

not lacking anything. James 1:2-4 NIV

A Sunday School student asked; *God is all powerful and can do anything, so why does God allow us, His children, to experience trials and hard times in our lives?*

Simple answer – God allows trials in our lives so we will grow stronger spiritually and to strengthen and test our faith.

In early days blacksmiths made harden steel from softer iron or lower grades of steel. They would place the iron into a hot furnace until it became red hot and soft enough to be formed. Then they would place the hot iron on an anvil and pound it into the desired shape using a big hammer. Next they plunged the still red hot iron into a bucket of cold water rapidly cooling the hot iron.

This cooling process caused impurities in the iron to separate from the iron and float on top of the water. The blacksmith skims the impurities from the top of the water and cast them aside. Because the impurities were removed the iron became stronger and harder. The blacksmith repeated the whole cycle of heating, pounding and cooling until all the impurities are removed and the once soft iron became harden steel.

God places us into the hot furnace of trials and hardships to soften us up so we can be shaped and formed the way God wants us to be. Then God pulls us from the furnace and while we are still hot he begins to shape us. Next God gives us a cooling off period so the impurities can come out. Some of us are so full of sinful impurities God has to repeat the process many times during our life.

Can you even imagine what a traumatic trial it was for Abraham when God tested his faith by asking him to sacrifice his only son, Isaac, as a burnt offering? (Genesis 22:2). After Abraham passed the test God blessed him richly. (Genesis 22:12-18). Because of this testing Abraham's faith became stronger because he knew that God was faithful in His promises.

The testing was really for Abraham's benefit, God already knew the out come of the testing. Abraham had just been put into the fire, pounded, and cooled. Some impurities of sinful doubt were removed from Abraham through the testing process.

Like Abraham, we all are tested and made stronger through trials and hardships. We may lose jobs and face financial ruin only to have God provide a better job when seemingly no jobs were available. Perhaps we or a loved one suffered from a serious illness and doctors proclaimed there was no cure but God sent his healing mercies and removed the illness.

Each time we witness God working in our lives to deliver us from these trials it strengthens our faith making us stronger in our walk with God. We just have to remember God's words; *So do not fear...I will uphold you with my righteous right hand. (Isaiah 41:10 NIV).*

Just as our physical bodies grow stronger from exercise so does our spiritual bodies. We lift heavy weights to test and strengthen our muscles and make our bodies stronger. God does the same for us by sending trials and hardships to test and strengthen our spiritual bodies, making then stronger so we can stand up to the temptations that Satan sends to attack us every day.

So you see trials are really blessings from God. We cannot recognize these blessing until our faith has become strong enough for us to see God's glory in the trials. Only when we realize that if we call on God he will answer our prayer and deliver us from our trials do we begin to grow in wisdom. Then we begin to understand why God sends these trials into our lives.

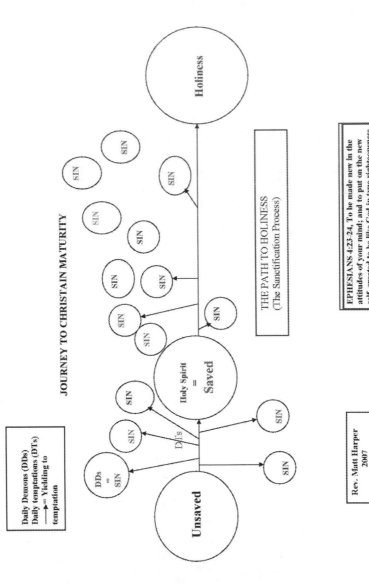

Figure one

CONTROLLING PERSONAL DEMONS

DEMON OF SIN INDUCING ANGER

In your anger do not sin...do not give

the devil a foot hold. Eph. 4:26-27.

Anger is one of our many emotions. There is nothing inherently bad about feeling angry it is just a natural response to an offensive act and a part of our defense system. In the Old Testament God became angry with His people many times and Jesus showed his anger with the moneychangers in the temple (John 2:14-16). However, how we respond to the offensive act could very well be sinful. There is an old saying: "success occurs when ability and opportunity meet."

Anger opens a door of opportunity to sin and Satan's demons are ready and able to pull you in that door and help you succeed in sinning, Ephesians 4:26&27, *In your anger do not sin...do not give the devil a foothold.* There are two elements to a person's anger mechanism that determines how a person will respond to an anger attack; inherent anger disposition, *call this attitude*, and learned anger disposition, *call this wisdom.*

1. **Inherent anger disposition (attitude):** This is a person's natural attitude and response towards things that generates anger emotions in them. For example, there are people who have a "short fuse" and become enraged and go into a defensive mode with very little provocation. At the other

end of the spectrum we have the "mellow fellow" who is very slow to respond to things that would anger most people.

2. **Learned anger disposition (wisdom):** This is a combination of inherent anger disposition and learned wisdom. For example a small man with a hot temper lives next door to a very large man with a dog that makes potty on the small man's lawn. Each time this happened there would be a physical altercation and the small man would end up in the emergency room. After a while the small man learned to call the police and let them handle the matter. Learned wisdom changed his inherent disposition into a new learned disposition.

The Daily Demons will have many opportunities to control your actions, if you are a "short fuse" person and respond from your inherent disposition. The Daily Demons will drive you to do and say all manner of things that will not be pleasing to God or good for your health, future, or reputation. These types of out of control, negative anger responses always lead to regret.

Controlling the anger demon: *He guides the humble in what is right and teaches them His ways. Psalms 25:9 NIV.* Key to responding to an offensive act is to never let yourself be tempted into saying or doing ugly sinful things. If necessary, walk away from the situation giving yourself time to relax and cool off, and then consider the best approach in resolving the matter. Learn to be humble but firm and persistent in your response but not sinful. For example the small man in the above paragraph could talk with his large neighbor and ask him to please curb his dog. If this fails he could talk with him again telling him officials will be called if the dog is not curbed. This is a much better response, no sinning and no visit to the emergency room.

How can you change yourself so you will not be a *short fuse* person? By having good things on the inside of you so good things will come out. Remember the sponge we spoke of earlier? Imagine you are that sponge and just like the sponge when you are under pressure whatever is on the inside comes out. If you are full of dirty water (hate, envy, grudges, jealousy, prejudices, etc.) when you come under pressure, such as a neighbor with a wayward dog, a lot of dirty water (Cussing, fighting, suing, etc.) comes out.

However, when you have a proper relationship with God your life will be guided by the Holy Spirit. Galatians Chapter 5 verses 16 through 26, with emphasis on verses 22 and 23, *But the fruit of the Spirit is love, joy, peace, patience, kindness, goodness, faithfulness, gentleness, and self-control.* When our lives are controlled by the Holy Spirit our sponge is filled with the clean and pure living water of Christ. Therefore we do not respond to pressure with dirty water, we respond with the fruit of the Holy Spirit. We have to continuously work hard to let go of and clean out all the ugly and sinful things that fill our soul so God can fill our sponge with His Living Water. Then we will not fall to the temptations to sin in our anger.

DEMON OF SELF-HATE

Love the Lord thy God with all your heart and

with all your soul and with all your mind. This is

first and greatest commandment, and the second

is like it, Love your neighbor as yourself.

Matt 22:37-39 NIV.

Ask any group of people if they love themselves and most of them would answer in the affirmative. This would not be a surprise; after all preserving and caring for oneself is a basic and natural instinct. One of the great commandments in the Bible is contingent upon loving one self.

We have many experiences in our lives some good and some bad. The good things we reflect on with fond memories and joy. However, the bad things have potential to create many problems in our lives. Some people have an innate propensity to record their every failure in their mind and continually replay these failures.

The demon of self-hate recognizes this area of weakness and mounts an attack on your Spirit. Without intervention this attack can drive you from being mildly unhappy with yourself to continuous self-hatred, deep depression and possibly self-destructive acts.

Many years ago I was in line for a promotion that I felt would have been and opportunity to send my career into high gear. When I did not get the promotion I was dismayed, puzzled, angry and very disappointed. I had invested many hours after work to earn advanced degrees, I excelled at every task assigned, and every year I received several bonuses for excellence.

I had covered every base and filled every square. How could I not get the promotion? The demon of self-hate began to attack my Faith. If God is just and loving, why was a less qualified person given the job? What did I do wrong? What didn't I do right? Who did I make angry?

Lord, show me what sin(s) I have committed! Why was I incapable of making the right moves to advance my career? In my mind, I had somehow failed in my quest for that *critical* promotion. I was not happy with myself and I began to doubt my abilities.

Then a Guardian Angel, my wife, reminded me to pray. I have to make a point here. You see Satan had so distracted me I had even forgotten the basic survival act – go to God in prayer. Once I turned it over to God, good-bye self-hate demon.

A year later I was in a far superior position, ten fold better than the sought after one in every way. The new position took us to California where God gave us opportunities to serve Him in wonderful ways we could never imagine. We spent the most exciting ten years of our lives there meeting and helping scores of God's people. California is such a beautiful place. My wife and I joke that when God made the earth he was almost finish and had lots of parts left over such as mountains, seashores, dessert, Redwoods, and He used them to create California.

Think of the world as a very large chessboard. Everyone in the world is a piece on the chessboard. God is the Chess Master. He knows the right time to move the right piece to the right place every time, all six billion or more pieces. *And we know that in all things God works for the good of those who love Him, who have been called according to His purpose. Ro 8:28. NIV.*

There is a time for everything, and a season for every activity under heaven Ecc 3:1. NIV. It is not our schedule that will prevail but God's. *Wait for the Lord, be strong and take heart and wait for the Lord. Ps 27:14 NIV.* God truly is the Chess Master and Master of all.

We are all God's creation and all He created is good. *God saw all that he had made, and it was very good.... Gen. 1:31 NIV.* The things we do are not always good, but we are good. Some of us do things that are so bad they are unspeakable. This is because we are all sinners and we do sinful things. We are not bad; it's the sinful things that we do. We should hate the sin and love the sinner, just as God does, because we are God's creations and we are good. We must remember to apply this rule to ourselves and love ourselves even when we do bad things, including our *failures.*

Controlling the self-hate demon: Turn off the tapes of bad things past, think of the good things you have achieved and done in your life. Think of the many good things you will do. *Finally brothers, whatever is good think about such things. Ph 4:8 NIV.* Satan's demons will try to guide you into a downward path of self-hate and destruction by playing and re-playing all the negative things that happened in your past over and over in your mind. Let those things go, leave them in the past.

Focus on the good things to come. *Forgetting what is behind and straining towards what is ahead, I press on towards the goal to win the prize for which God has called me...in Christ Jesus. Ph 3:13-14 NIV.*

Remember, God knows all your sins and He knows you will sin again, but He still loves you. All God asks is for you to ask for forgiveness, repent and turn away from your sins. Surely you can do this simple act for yourself. Forgive yourself and turn away from the demon of self-hate. Defeat this demon by giving yourself another chance to follow Christ and do the right things. God will lead if you will follow Him.

THE IT DEMON

Do not store up treasures on earth

where moth and rust destroy.

Matthew 6:19

And I saw that all labor and all achievement

spring from man's envy of his neighbor. This

too is meaningless, a chasing after the wind

Ecclesiastes 4:4 NIV

Many times you have heard people say; *boy, that guy really has it made, if you keep working hard one day you will make it, or you have to go to college if you want to make it in this world.* Have you every stopped to consider what the heck IT really is? Will you know it when you make IT, find IT or get IT? Many people today are working so hard to capture IT that they run over IT in their pursuit of "IT" and never even recognized IT.

A pastor was talking to children in a first year Sunday school class and he asked several children what they thought of the human race. He got a couple of expected answers then a little girl responded by saying; *I want to win it.* The pastor, puzzled by her response, asked what she meant. The little girl said; *I'm going to run very fast and beat all the other humans to the finish line and I'll be the winner.* Many people look at life in a similar fashion.

They work very hard to acquire the most things so they will win the human race. There was a popular bumper sticker in the 1980s that read: *he who dies with the most toys wins the race.* Seems a lot of people are still thinking that way. For a lot of people enough can never be enough, they are on a relentless, never ending journey to reach the finish line and win the human race. They become so obsessed with running and winning this race they fail to live and appreciate life. They never make the starter house into a loving home because they are too busy working to "make IT" and move the family into a better house in a nicer neighborhood. Then they are blessed with success in their business or career and they have to move up to a house in the right part of town so their peers will know they are making IT. Simply does not matter that they never got around to making and enjoying a loving home or establishing good family and community relations in any of the trophy houses they lived in.

These people don't understand the true objective of the human race, which is not to win it but to be a constructive part of it while helping each other along the way. They will continue to seek lasting joy, peace and fulfillment all the days of their lives and never find it. Why, because they continue to worship and give things first place in their lives in place of God.

God gave his people these commands in Exodus chapter 20 verses two and three: *I am the Lord your God, who brought you out of Egypt, out of the land of slavery. You shall have no other gods before me.* The people disobeyed God when they were wandering in the desert and they continue to disobey Him now.

God continues to bless them by allowing them to

have stuff and many of them in turn worshipped the stuff and made it their god by giving the stuff first place in their lives. Instead of going to church and giving thanks to God for His blessing, they go to a NFL football game to impress their friends with their new stuff that God has blessed them with.

However, they never acknowledge God's role in their having the stuff. What has happened here is they no longer have the stuff, rather the stuff has control of them. The stuff has become their "god", and that is a very bad situation to be in. Always keep God first in your life that way you will always control the stuff in your life. **Remember, you have the stuff, don't let the stuff have you.**

This is how the Daily Demons trick us; they lead us to seek IT in the form of material things. Ecclesiastes 5:10, *whoever loves money never has money enough.* The IT that can satisfy our need for fulfillment and end our seeking can never be found in material things. Let's take "IT" and divide it into three classes, physical IT, emotional IT and spiritual IT.

Physical IT- This IT consist of material things such as houses, cars, HDTVs, diamonds and any thing that caters to the flesh. We could find a comfortable level of physical IT and be content, once our needs are met, if we did not have to contend with the next IT which is the emotional IT.

Emotional IT- This IT is the one that creates so much turmoil in our lives. Envy is a big factor in this "IT". Envy always try to disturb our peace. *...All labor and achievement springs from man's envy of his neighbor. Ecc. 4:4 NIV.* For example, we may have established a suitable physical IT, nice house, reliable car, adequate income and life is good. Then a neighbor buys a new and expensive car that is much nicer than ours. Envy gets into our heart and our physical IT is no longer satisfied. In order to restore our peace we must have a car that is equal to or better than our neighbors. And so it goes when we enter into the human race to win it all. Enough will never be enough. There are many demons working in the emotional IT that disturbs our peace; there is envy, greed, jealousy, hate and several more. Each demon works towards the same goal and that is to deny us the peace and joy we so desperately seek.

Spiritual IT- Many years ago Wendy's Hamburgers had a commercial and the catch phrase was: *"Where's the beef?"* Well, the Spiritual IT is the beef, it's the real deal, and it's what we are looking for. When our spiritual IT is in proper order we live by the fruit of that spirit; love, joy, peace, patience, kindness, goodness, faithfulness, gentleness, and self-control. We will no longer be tempted by the sinful nature with it's passions and evil desires. *Turn everything over to God and he will give you peace, which transcends all understanding, and you can be content (at peace) whatever the circumstances. . Philippians 4:6-7 &11 NIV.* When we accept Jesus Christ as our savior and keep God first in our lives we no longer seek to find peace in worldly things.

Controlling the IT demon:

Step one: Put God at the head of your life. Have no other god before Him, not your job, house, car or anything else.

Step two: Build up your Spiritual IT and it will keep your physical and emotional IT demons, with their evil temptations, under control.

Step three: When you can understand that the family, not the number of square feet in a house, determines if that house will be a warm, nurturing and loving place you are controlling the IT Demons.

Step four: When you understand your relationship

with God is the most important relationship in your life, you are controlling the IT demons.

When your hard working neighbor or co-worker is rewarded for their efforts, wish them well with a loving heart free of envy or jealousy. Do not compare your blessings with your neighbor's blessings. Be content with what God has given you and trust Him to guide your life to meet His will and purpose and God will prosper you and give you joy, peace and eternal life. Remember, joy peace, happiness and true worth is not determined or measured by the stuff we have but rather by who we are in the sight of God.

Remember, you have the stuff, don't let the stuff have you.

DEMON OF PREJUDICE

God does not show favoritism but accepts

men from every nation who fear Him and

do what is right. Acts 10: 34-35.

The meaning of prejudice is to prejudge. Prejudice is an attitude taken towards an individual without adequate factual basis or understanding. Because some people have prejudice attitudes that are negative towards certain individuals or groups they sometimes do things that are detrimental to them for no valid reason. Most often prejudiced attitudes are based on opinions generated by environmental influences in lieu of facts. When the attitudes we instill in our children are based on facts and truth they are less likely to be prejudice as adults.

Problem is too many people find it easy, convenient and socially comfortable living their lives based on prejudiced attitudes. By accepting the environmental influences around them they are in-turn accepted by the community at large. Stereotyping makes it even easier, you don't have to waste time considering facts about a particular place, person or group.

For example, if a house is in a given zip code you assume, based on your opinion, it can have only limited value. If a person belongs to a certain group they could never have the understand or skills required to contribute to and play a meaningful role in society.

When we see a strange person that is dirty, smelly, who appears to be under the influence of drugs or alcohol we should not pass judgment on that person. Because that person is a stranger to us we don't know how they can to be in their current state. Our initial feelings should be caution, concern and compassion. We should never allow our hearts to become callused towards one of God's creations through prejudice and stereotyping. However, if a person behaves in a threatening, abusive or otherwise ungodly manner towards us we have no choice but to consider him for what he has demonstrated himself to be and conduct our self accordingly.

The demon of prejudice tempts us with the warm embraces of acceptance. We are all social creatures that needs to feel wanted and accepted by our communities. Our reputations determine our acceptance and standing in the community and are to be guarded and defended at all times. Not wanting to be at odds with our community some of us adopt or tolerate their attitudes, factual or otherwise.

In some cases we let our quest to maintain a high standing in our community determine where we go out to dine, worship, socialize, and even where our children attend school. We dare not risk being tainted by getting to close to the wrong people.

Sometimes people or communities are exposed for what they are and individuals will have to decide if they will support the truth or yield to temptation and continue to live a lie. *Is Ronnie, our Youth Minister, really a child molester? How could that be? He lives in a great zip code? To report the allegations and risk a public investigation that would reflect poorly on our church and com-*

munity is a hard decision. Maybe those ten children were mistaken.

After all Ronnie is the poster boy of Youth Ministers. He has been a Youth Minister at several churches over the past few years. He is handsome, cheerful and polite there is just no way he could do something that awful.. This is a good example of someone showing prejudice to deny something that does not fit his or her opinion of what should be. Perhaps Ronnie was selected to be Youth Minister over another candidate that was not handsome, cheerful and polite. The candidate was not the *right person* for the job. If the selecting party had checked Ronnie's background, which they did not because in their opinion *Ronnie was the right kind of person,* they would have discovered his three prior convictions for child molestation. They would have known the truth and not have been deceived by the demon of prejudice.

People that look to truth for answers will never be blinded by opinions.

We have no way of knowing who a person is inside. Only God knows that.   He even knows things about us that we don't know. We don't always fully understand how or why we react a certain way in a given situation. On occasions I have asked myself *why I reacted like that.* My reaction was a surprise to me but not to God.

God fully understands the good and the bad inside each of us. Some of us had ugly notions and opinions bored into our minds at an early age and they remained tucked way in our soul. If we grow and develop properly, we begin to realize these ugly notions are false and we strive to replace them with attitudes based on truth. If we have a strong desire to we can generally conduct our lives in sane and rational ways. We comply with the legal, traditional and social rules of order that govern us.

We refrain from saying or doing prejudicial things that would be harmful or offensive to anyone or any entity.

However in times of stress and compulsion we will be tempted to fall into the easy and comfortable arms of prejudicial attitudes and or actions.

In the interest of balance we must discuss the issue of good judgment vs. prejudice. If someone is a member of a group that has a history of bad behavior, your good judgment will tell you to exercise caution in dealing with that person. Not due to any prejudice against the individual but based on the facts of the groups history.

God gave us the gift of discernment and we should always use that gift to guide us in our actions. I feel the need to repeat a key point *use caution in dealing with that person* do not prejudge the person. Sometimes there can be reasons beyond their control why a good person gets involved with a bad group or find themselves in a bad situation.

Controlling the prejudice demon: In a word, communicate. Get to know as much as you can about the people, places or things you are prejudice against. *Do not judge, or you to will be judged ...why do you look at the speck of sawdust in your brother's eye but pay no attention to the plank in your own eye? Matt. 7:1-3 NIV.* Examine yourself to determine if you have prejudice feelings towards certain individuals or groups.

If you feel uncomfortable in their presences ask yourself if there is some objective reason why you feel this way. If you can identify no objective reason for your feelings, ugly notions and opinions from your childhood could be the root of your feelings.

Ignorance is the fuel of prejudice and it can create and pass along wildfires of hatred, anger, division and destruction for many generations. Truth is the antidote for ignorance and the road to truth is communications.

When you indulge in an act of prejudice, force yourself to learn from it. Have a talk with yourself and examine your thinking and discover the true reason why you chose to commit that act of prejudice. Were there some environmental influences in your life that instilled these ugly notions and opinions in your personality?

Deciding to communicate with and understand people, groups and situations and then interacting with them based on know factual truths rather then reacting to emotions driven by ugly notions and opinions is the key to controlling the demon of prejudice.

DEMON OF LAZINESS

Lazy hands make a man poor, but

diligent hands bring wealth

Proverbs 10:4

If a man will not work, he shall not eat.

2 Th. 3:10

"This Power-Water drink is great," Jill excitedly declared to her mother as she swooped into the kitchen. "Do you know it has several vitamins that gives you energy and keeps your body strong? Someone had a great idea and I'm sure they made a fortune with this new product." Jill's father, Edward began to do a slow burn as he sat in his recliner thinking of all the profits he would not get because he did not act sooner.

Edward thought of this idea several years ago and even developed a recipe for a vitamin enriched water drink almost identical to Power-Water. However Edward never got around to applying for a patent for his recipe. It seems he could never find the time and energy to do the difficult and time-consuming research and file the, in Edwards words *complicated* and *un-necessary,* paperwork required to protect his recipe.

Laziness leads to poverty, *Lazy hands make a man poor, but diligent hands bring wealth. Pr. 10:4 NIV.* The demon of laziness had inflected Edward with lazy hands causing him to miss a great opportunity.

Investing our time wisely always pays handsome dividends. It was early autumn when I used our family garden to illustrate this notion to our young children. We worked hard in the spring tilling the soil, planting seeds, adding insecticides and fertilizers and pulling weeds as the garden grew. Slowly we began to see the results of all that hard work as the first buds slowly emerged. The summer rains coaxed out a dazzling array of color as a multitude of blossoms burst out from each plant. The garden produced an abundance of vegetables and we watched as each one grew throughout the season. We had enough vegetables to meet our needs and share with our neighbors. We were able to preserve some vegetables for the winter.

We had diligent hands. In contrast, one of our neighbors, Mr. Ted, did nothing to prepare his garden and spent no time maintaining it. He simply dug holes, planted seeds and the garden was done. Not surprising, Mr. Ted got very little produce from his garden. Mr. Ted had lazy hands.

Life is like a garden; you have to invest much hard work in the early years of your life to get a good harvest in the latter years. Doctors, engineers, electricians, pilots, plumbers and lawyers discipline themselves to spend many of their early years attending schools and training.

This is hard work requiring much sacrifice. However, in the summer of their lives their gardens (businesses/professions) begin to blossom and yield much fruit. They will have more then enough fruit to last them into the autumn and winter (retirement) years of their lives. They had diligent hands.

Laziness can and will greatly influence every aspect

of our lives. Are we too lazy to spend time with our children showing them we care and helping them develop into well-rounded adults? Has the demon of laziness strapped us to our cozy recliners and molded remotes to our hands so we spend our lives mindlessly glaring at a television screen?

We no longer have the opportunity to meet and talk to our neighbors when we drive home because we now have remote garage door openers. We just push the button, swish into the garage and push the button again closing the doors to the garage and to any neighborly relations.

We may call this the benefits of modern conveniences, but bottom-line, it's laziness. Half of our population is overweight from laziness. Children no longer mow the lawn because we have a yard person. These children miss the opportunities to learn the relationship between work and rewards and the value and satisfaction of earning a few dollars. Plus they miss the benefits of exercising their bodies while doing meaningful work.

Look at the ant, you lazy person, consider its ways and be wise! It has no boss, no overseer or ruler, yet it stores its provisions in summer and gathers its food at harvest. How long will you lay there, you sluggard? When will you get up from your sleep? A little sleep, a little slumber, a little folding of hands to rest and poverty will come on you like a bandit and scarcity like an armed man Pr.6: 6-11 NIV.

Laziness is a learned behavior like so many other things in our lives. Lazy parents, by example, influence their children to be lazy.

Lazy parents that do not help, support and encourage their children in their school activities and homework, knowingly or unknowingly, contribute to their children failing in school. Without a solid education these young people will find it more difficult to succeed in life. Some people call laziness procrastination however, results are the same; things that need to be done don't get done.

The longer we put off doing what needs to be done the bigger the problem becomes. Four years ago you noticed paint was peeling in several areas around your house but you did nothing. Now you have to pay five times as much to repair the damage wood and repaint the house.

You had a heated argument with a co-worker last year and you later discovered you were wrong and you planned to make things right by apologizing but you never got around to it.

This week that same co-worker got promoted and is now your new boss.

If you allow yourself to become too lazy to do the things required to live a productive and meaningful life you will surly have an existence marked only by a series of failures.

The demon of laziness is on a mission to destroy you by attacking your sense of self worth. If your laziness can prevent you from accomplishing anything positive in your life it will be hard to feel good about yourself. When this negative self image dominates your thinking you can't have respect and love for yourself or others. This is exactly the position the demon of laziness want you to be in. From here it will be easy for him to drive you into a state of utter hopelessness and to ultimately crush your spirit and your will to live.

Get up and get busy. Resist the demon of laziness, don't let him have the victory in you life. Never forget, for every demon we have the antidote, our Lord and savior Jesus Christ who sent His Holy Spirit to deliver us.

Controlling the demon of laziness: My Grandfather

told me many years ago: "Don't put off until tomorrow what you can and need to do today!" and it has proven to be very prudent. Since laziness is a learned behavior we can unlearn it.

As in all things go to God first in prayer and He will guide you in effecting changes in your life. Here are some steps that will help you on journey to change:

- Step one: Stay away from lazy people, you don't need their negative influences.

- Step two: Make a decision to not put off doing things that can and need to be done today.

- Step three: Make it your goal to do two things today you would have normally deferred until a later date.

- Step four: List things that need to be done, one list for home, one for work and another for social and recreational activities. Set a date that you will complete the task and stick to that date.

- Step five: Gradually increase the number of things you will NOT put off until you reach the point where you routinely do everything that can and need to be done each day.

This may sound simple and it really is. Knowing the right thing to do usually is simple. The difficult part is having the self-discipline and perseverance to do what is simply right. The longer you work at it the easier and more rewarding it becomes.

DEMON OF THINGS PAST

Brothers I do not consider myself yet to have taken hold of it. But one thing I do: Forgetting what is behind and straining towards what is ahead.

Philippians 3:13

Many are the times when a word, act or scene unlocks the dreaded gate to the dark and ugly pits of negative memories of things past. Suddenly the ten-ton demon of things past charges to the forefront of your mind crushing peace, joy, happiness, security, and confidence under the smothering weight of his crippling presence.

A failed business, a marriage ending in a bitter divorce, all the horrors of an addicted life, deceit exposed in a trusted friendship and bitter disappointments of many kinds are the types of memories that can pull and stretch the fabric of our souls. Satan attacks us with these ugly memories of things past trying to crush our spirits and destroy our will to press on to a new time and a better place

Brothers, I do not consider myself yet to have taken hold of it. But one thing I do: Forgetting what is behind and straining towards what is ahead, I press on towards the goal to win the prize for which God has called me heavenward in Jesus Christ. Php. 3:13-14 NIV.

Trickzie was a young, strong and beautiful English bulldog. She was very loving, loyal and obedient and most of all she was my best friend. I was five to seven years of age living on a farm with my grandparents in a small South Carolina town.

During those times farmers took a very dim view of dogs that would not hunt, had the mange, ate chicken eggs, or worst yet ate chickens. These were considered bad or useless dogs and it was considered the farmer's duty to dispose of them. My grandfather had a very crude method of getting rid of useless dogs. He would use a rope to hang them by their hind legs in our pecan tree. Then he would dig a deep hole under them, shoot them with his 12 gauge shotgun, cut them down, pour lime on the body and cover the hole.

I had helped him perform this process several times. One summer I went away to visit my mother and when I returned I learned grandpa had caught Trickzie eating one of his chickens and had disposed of her.

Grandpa took away a lot from me when he killed Trickzie, he took my best friend but far worst he took away the sense of trust and confidence I had developed in him and people in general. I also lost the security I had felt in believing what was mine was going to remain mine.

This act instilled in me an insecurity and lack of trust that has followed me throughout my life and remains with me in my years of retirement. I feel the need to have two of everything; if I lose one "bulldog" again I'll have a backup. I can only find a sense of security in redundancy. I am very cynical when meeting new people and it takes a very long time for me to trust anyone.

I feel they will eventually betray any trust we may develop, just as my Grandpa did. This puts a cloud on relationships because people can somehow sense when you don't trust them.

I shared this story from my past to illustrate how powerful and long lasting the demon of things past can be, and how difficult they are to control. It took me more than 50 years to realize the source of this demon, and I discovered it accidentally.

Some children from our church were interviewing senior members and during my interview the young person asked what was my fondest childhood memory and then what was my worst childhood memory and I related the above story as my worst memory. I was shocked to hear myself respond with that story. I was actually surprised how vividly I remembered the story and how sad telling it still made me feel. I learned a lot about myself that day. I began to understand so many things better; I thank God for sending those children.

. Bad memories can result from the actions of other, such as the case with my Grandpa but most often they result from our poor decisions. These bad decisions can impact ours lives in one of two ways; we can learn from our mistake, grow and move on or our mistakes can haunt and cripple us for many years sometimes with negative and damaging consequences.

Some young people, in their quest to be popular, begin to "experiment" with drugs. Once addicted they go into a physical and mental freefall spiraling downwards until reaching the very bottom pits of human existence. After reaching bottom a fortunate few somehow manage to break free of their additions and begin the process of restoring themselves to some level of functional ability. At this juncture in their lives what these people need is support and encouragement to continue on their road to recovery.

However, this is the time when demons of things past

use relatives and acquaintances to remind and condemn them of their sins, failures and all negative things associated with their past addictions. What these judgmental people fail to understand is, an addicted person is not always a bad person. Sometimes an addicted person is a really good person with a very bad problem that is controlling their life.

Like wise a failed business or failed marriage does not equate to a failed person. There can be countless reasons for failures in life all having nothing to do with a person's character, abilities or worth. Many opportunities for good relationships and business adventures are ruined when a person becomes paralyzed by negative memories of things past and cannot let go and embrace the present and look to the future.

Those evil daily demons lurking in shadows are always waiting to record and capitalize on our failures. In our times of vulnerability these memories of past failures tempts us to give up, withdraw and wallow in self-pity and despair. Left unchecked negative memories lead to fears and doubts that blinds us to future opportunities.

Learn and grow from your mistakes and only save memories that will help you avoid making the same mistakes again. Mistakes are life's way of giving you the opportunity to get up, grow up, wise up and build up faith, strength and character. When God is in our life, we should not fear anything. *For God did not give us a Spirit of fear or timidity, but a Spirit of power, of love and of self-discipline. 2 Tim. 1:7 NIV.*

Controlling the demon of things past: *Behold, I will create new heavens and a new earth. The former things will not be remembered nor will they come to mind. Isa. 65:17 NIV.*

Stay away from people and places that remind you of negative experiences. If you can't avoid some of these people, such as family members or co-workers, be firm in telling them you are moving on with your life and prefer focusing on the present and future while not discussing negative issues and events of the past.

We can avoid some people and places but we cannot avoid ourselves and often we are our own worst enemy when dealing with our past. Instead of using our free time to focus on positive things we allow our mind to meditate on negative memories.

There is an old saying; *An idle mind is the devil's workshop.* Keep busy. Use your free time to do something constructive. Find a new hobby, visit the elderly and sick, or get a part-time job. Do whatever you can to avoid long periods of idleness. Those daily demons are quick to declare open warfare on an idle mind.

When you are idle the demon of things past will attempt to recall every failure, every negative thing you ever did and every negative thing anyone ever did or said to you in your life. Soon you will harbor contempt for yourself, everyone around you and everything you ever did in life. That's a very defeating and depressing situation. You cannot and do not want to live this way.

Each day is full of new opportunities for those that can see them. Don't let memories of negative experiences from the past rob you of your joy today, crush your dreams, and steal your visions of better things to come. You are God's creation and made in His image; you are precious in His sight. God loves you and he can and will forgive you.

Why not forgive yourself and put the past to rest? Regardless of who you were, what you did and how long you did it you are still a child of God. You can still do anything and be anybody you desire to be with God's help. *I can do everything through him who gives me strength. Php. 4:13 NIV.*

DEMON OF FEAR

Don't be afraid I am with you...I will uphold

you with my mighty right hand.

Isaiah 41:10

Demons of fear, self-hate, and things past are closely related because they all use memories of bad experiences to attack our mind and spirit. Memory is a God given gift we can and should use to gain knowledge and grow in wisdom. With memory we could do a task as simple as operating a flashlight or perform complicated procedures such as brain surgery.

Satan leads us to use our memory in counter-productive ways by storing away negative experiences. Memories of bad experiences instill fear and fear can be crippling or totally debilitating.

Early one Saturday morning in December, our youngest child was abruptly awakened by the sounds of a fire truck. She was frightened because, in her mind, a fire truck meant someone's home was burning. Looking through her window she saw Santa Clause sitting on top of a fire truck. Her four-year-old brain recorded a fear of Santa Clause associated with burning homes.

However, Santa was really tossing Christmas candy to children in the street. She is now a very successful school principal that still refuses to have any association with Santa Clause. Her fear of Santa cost her some joys of a childhood Christmas. There are certainly no pictures of her sitting on Santa's knee!

Fear in adults can be far more crippling than a lost relationship with Santa and the consequences of such fear are far more serious. For example only a very small percentage of the nation's population become business owners. There are often two things that stop people from becoming business owners; fear of failure and the unknown. People know someone or heard of someone who failed in their attempt to operate a business and there was much negative and ugly commentary from the naysayers and possibly heavy financial lost associated with the failure. These harsh memories of other people failures could cause fear in many people stopping them from attempting business ventures.

But when you live by faith you will have the courage to meet the challenge. Like everything else in life learning to run a successful business is a slow process. Sometimes you have to crawl before you walk, and then you can run. It can be frightful when you have little or no experience and you have to make a heavy financial commitment but faith, confidence and hard work will see you through.

We live in a time when large industries are being built on people's fears. People are being conditioned via the news media, marketing, and advertising channels to fear an ever-widening set of conditions and situations while these industries are linking an insurable risk with each new fear.

The insurance industry thrives on our fears of risk. We insure everything from automobiles to violins. We insure our homes and contents then we secure it with elaborate systems to avoid the risk of burglary. We insure our vacations against bad weather, and entertainers and sports figures insure their body parts. I sometimes wonder how long before someone will offer a policy insuring a person's Faith? If they did, little doubt they will have customers.

Over the past fifty 50 years the fear of responsibility has increased rapidly. As a child I was taught that **for every right there is a matching set of responsibilities**.

If you accepted the right, and rewards, of being a supervisor, you have to accept the associated responsibilities. It is becoming increasingly difficult to find employees willing to accept the roles of leadership because they are afraid of being accountable when things go wrong. As I see it, there are two key reasons for this fear: a self-perception of incompetence, real or not, and unwillingness to accept the consequences of failure. A lot of people lack the discipline to do the things required to acquire and effectively function in a leadership capacity. Therefore, they will continue to be fearful of assuming a leadership role.

What too many people fail to understand is the biggest, longest lasting and most regrettably failure is the failure to try.

Controlling the Demon of Fear: *So do not fear, for I am with you...I will uphold you with my righteous right hand. Isa. 41:10 NIV.* What a promise, much better then any insurance policy and no hidden clauses. Plus, God himself is the underwriter!

First step is to identify the things you fear the most in your life. These could be things you fear doing, people that intimidate you, making critical decisions or making a commitment,

Now select the top five or less fears on your list that are having the most negative impacts on your life.

Take a candid and objective look at each of these

fears spending time to determine why you fear them. Then ask yourself is this a logical fear. Most of our fears are ill founded, we just need to take time and analyze the situation.

For example to reduce risk when making critical decisions take time to do good research before deciding on a course of action. Remember the old adage; haste make waste. Often two people can reduce tension between them through communications, talking things out. Sometimes it may require a third party acting as a mediator. Don't let fear paralyze you, use fear as a motivator that drives you to resolve the issues causing the fear.

Walk with God and He will guide your path. *And we know that in all things God works for the good of those who love him, who have been called according to his purpose. Ro 8:28 NIV.*

Fear no one or no thing but, before starting any venture talk with God to be sure what you plan to do is in line with His will and purpose. Regardless of what you are planning to do; start a new job, relationship, business, buy a new home, the best way to increase the chances of success is to humbly ask God to work for the good of your plan. *He guides the humble in what is right and teaches them his ways. .Ps. 25:9 NIV.*

Live by Faith not by fear. *For God did not give us a Spirit of fear but a Spirit of power, of love and of self-discipline. 2 Tm 1:7 NIV.* Keep God first in your life and before doing anything go first to God in prayer and ask Him to guide your path.

DEMON OF NON-APPRECATION

Give thanks to the Lord, for He is good; His

love endures forever. I Chronicles 16:34 NIV

Let them give thanks to the Lord for His unfailing

love and His wonderful deeds for men, for

He satisfies the thirsty and fills the hungry

with good things. Psalms 107: 8-9 NIV

This **Demon of Non-Appreciation** works very diligently to focus our attention on all things negative and to blind us to the many blessings God gives us every day. This demon wants us to take God's blessings for granted, to accept them as being routine without embracing their great value. The demon's goal is to prevent or destroy our relationship with God.

Hopefully the following text will help you be more aware of how we fail to appreciate the things God does for us. Don't feel alone in this, we all are guilty at some times in our lives.

While you are reading this text has it occurred to you that being able to read is a blessing on several levels? First you are blessed to have vision; you were blessed when someone cared enough to teach you how to read; you are blessed because you have the ability to understand what you read; and lastly you have a desire to read.

Lack most of us you probably seldom, if ever, consider reading as anything more then a routine part of your daily activities, nothing we would pause and consciously appreciate. It's only when something, such as failing vision, threatens our ability to read that we consciously begin to appreciate what a great blessing the ability to read really is.

So it is with us in so many ways. We are so busy making a living we often forget to stop and enjoy the things God has blessed us with. God blesses us with a new house but do we take time to dedicate the house to God and thank him for the blessing?

Do we use that house to make a loving home for our family and neighbors to come together in fellowship? Do we really appreciate the house that God blessed us with or do we see it as just a stepping-stone to get to the next, bigger, house?

How would you feel if you gave one of your children and his/her mate a new house for a wedding gift and they never said thank you or invited you in? God feels the same way when we take His blessing for granted.

There was a teenage boy named Tommy who came from a middle class family and every week the father would give Tommy $75.00 for allowance. In the 1970's that was a very generous allowance and Tommy was the envy of all his friends.

Tommy's dad would allow him use of the family car on Saturday nights and this made Tommy very popular with his buddies and the girls. Because Tommy's dad was so generous with his children he could not afford to shop at the usual men stores, instead he would often pick up some things for himself at the dollar store. One day shortly before Father's Day Tommy's Mom reminded him that he should buy a nice gift for his father.

Tommy's dad was in the next room and he heard Tommy as he complained to his Mom that he was going to a hot party and had no money to spend on a gift for Dad. Tommy's Mom insisted and Tommy grudgingly agreed to buy a gift. However, Tommy assured his Mom it would not be much of a gift because he needed his allowance money for the party.

Dad opened his gift from Tommy on Father's Day and he immediately recognized the bundle of socks. They were the same ones he had looked at in the dollar store and decided they were too cheap even though there was ten pair in a bundle for one dollar, ten cents a pair.

Dad was very deeply hurt and disappointed that his son felt that his Father only deserved a bundle of ten-cent socks in appreciation for all the sacrifices he had made to provide a good life for his son.

How do you show God your appreciation? When you give an offering on Sunday, do you give God a pair of "ten cent socks"?

You have heard the expression 24/7, but not many people stop to do the math that equals 168 hours in a seven-day week. If God, our Father, is gracious enough to bless you with another 168 hours to live a healthy life, what gift would you be willing to give in return? Would you give Him ten percent of the time he gave you?

That would mean using 16.8 hours each week to serve and worship God. Truth is most of us have a difficult time spending even two hours on Sunday morning to attend church and honor God. Let's do that math again; Tommy spent one dollar out of 75 to give his Dad a gift, that's 1.3 percent of what his Dad blessed him with. If we give two hours out of the 168 hours our Father blessed us with that only equal 1.2 percent. Even Tommy is showing more appreciation then a lot of us Christians.

A woman can be loving, loyal, understanding, supportive, engaging and an all around great wife and wonderful mother to her five teenage children but her husband can only focus on the twenty pound she has gained over the past fifteen years. The demon of non-appreciation has blinded him to the point that he cannot or will not appreciate all the positive attributes of his wife. The husband is so busy judging his wife he cannot see the plank of non-appreciation in his own eye nor can he see the bulging beer belly he has developed.

Some families are blessed with wonderful, loving, helpful and obedient children. However, the children don't always manage to get good grades in school even though they do make every effort to improve. But the parents only focus on the poor grades and never show the children any appreciation for the good things they do. The demon is busy setting the stage for trouble ahead.

God sends his life giving rain and many people only complain because it spoils their weekend plans. They never stop to consider that without rain we would not have the beauty of all the trees and plants that gives life to the earth. Truth is many people never really take the time to appreciate the beauty of nature. To these unfortunate people the beauty of nature is treated just like background noise, it's there but they really never recognize it.

If you were unemployed and God provides you with a new job that's not equal in pay or status to your old job, **thank God for giving you a new job**! If you show God you appreciate what he did for you he will do more for you. **Keep God first and you will never be last!**

There are many things we should show our appreciation for each day; being alive, sound minds, food, shelter and the list goes on. We have to keep our minds focused on the positive aspect of the things that come our way and keep the demon of non-appreciation at bay.

Controlling the demon of non-appreciation. Many people cannot appreciate all the good things that happen in their lives. Often this is because their hearts and minds are totally focused on acquiring more stuff. They simply never take time to smell the roses. **Fortunate is he who knows how to make a living. Blessed is he who knows how to make a life.** In their rush to win the human race they have become hardened and they only focus on the negative aspects of every circumstance. The goal is to change to a positive outlook. Practice looking to see the good in every situation, learn to appreciate and enhance that good. We may have to slow our pace a bit and get in step with the rhythm of our natural surroundings before we can begin to recognize Gods manifold blessings.

Just remember, it took us many years to develop our blindness to God's blessings and it will take some time to learn how to recognize and appreciate them again. As in all things we should go to God in prayer asking him to open our eyes and our minds that we may see and receive his many blessings. Then we must thank God and give him all the glory for his goodness. *Give thanks in all circumstances, for this is God's will for you in Christ Jesus. I Th. 5:18 NIV.*

If a person cannot or will not recognize and appreciate their own positive attributes it generally follows that they will not have much appreciation for anyone or anything else. Therefore, the first step in learning to appreciate your circumstances is learning to appreciate oneself. How do you feel about yourself? Is the demon of self-hate busy in your life?

Sometimes we have to be our own booster club and give a shout out for the good things we do. Think positive thoughts about yourself. Don't be vain but do focus on and recognize your positive qualities and achievements. If you are a Christian that means you are a child of God and that alone makes you a very special, loved and valuable person. Far too many Christians suffer from low esteem, depression and other maladies because they have lost focus and allowed themselves to wander away from their relationship with God.

It's at this point that Satan sends his demons to attack with full fury. Our attitude becomes negative and we become callused to the blessings around us and we recognizing none of them.

In short, look for the positive in everyone, everything and all circumstances. When you find it, appreciate it.

DEMON OF SIN ACCLIMATION

If sinners entice you do not give in to them

Proverbs 1:10 NIV

And lead us not into temptation

but delivery us from evil

Matthew 6:13 NIV

There is an old story that was told to me a long time ago about frogs. As the story goes you can place a frog in a pan of water, on a stove and slowly increase the heat until the water boils and the frog will just adjust to the heat and never leap out of the pan. Story says the frog will stay right there in the pan and cook to death. I would never be so cruel as to try and prove this old story but the story makes a good point.

You see, that's the way some people are with sin, it can be burning all around them and they never leap out of it. They just adjust and get used to it and eventually it consumes them and they die a spiritual death and eventually burn in hell. Let me tell you a little story about that.

We gasped for fresh air as we desperately tried to rip off the gas masks covering our faces. Burning eyes runny noses and stinging skin were the results of not following instructions. The drill sergeant had tool us to be very careful when putting on our gas mask as they were the only thing between us and the simulated nerve gas that would be released in the area.

He told us if we failed to fit the mask properly the gas would be able to get in and attack our nervous system through our eyes, nose, ears and throat. The drill sergeant also explained that in a real war zone **allowing even the smallest amount** of the gas to get inside our system would be deadly because unlike the simulated nerve gas the real gas would kill you very quickly.

The real gas is often designed so that it will be very hard to detect usually with very little odor or color. Therefore we were taught how to recognize the subtle signs that told us nerve gas was present so we could put on our mask to protect ourselves. We were also taught how to check our mask to ensure the seals were in good working condition so they would provide a good shield against the gas.

We also had chemical warfare suits that offered protection against various deadly chemicals and they also required frequent checking to ensure they were in good working order. In a war zone our lives could very well depend on the proper functioning of this equipment.

Sin works very much like the nerve gas, it can seep into our lives ALMOST undetected and before we realize it sin will have gained a strong grip on our lives. I use the word almost because, being Christians, we know when we have done something wrong, there is always that little twinge of guilt but sometimes we just shrug it off and continue in our mischief.

We know if we taste one grape in the supermarket it's sampling if we taste ten grapes that's grazing and it's a sin. And if we yield to grape grazing next we will be back for lunch. That's the way sin works, it pulls us in a little at a time. It gives us time to acclimate to a seemingly harmless sin before tempting us with increasingly serious sins. That's why all sin is serious! Indulging in what may appear to be harmless sin can eventually lead to spiritual death.

Regardless if it's drug addiction, adultery, embezzlement or alcohol abuse sin works by gradually getting people addicted to it. First sin attracts people by appealing to their evil desires. Satan knows the desires of our hearts and he will gladly present that desire in an attractively wrapped, seemingly harmless package.

You may not know what sins are your weaknesses but Satan does and he knows when you are most vulnerable to them. If stealing is one of your weaknesses a simple thing like a paper clip could be used to entice you to commit that first act of thievery. You're at work and need to clip some personal papers together so you look in the desk and find a paper clip. A little voice tells you the clip is not yours but you tell yourself it's a big company and they will not miss one paper clip and you are right the company probably will not miss the paper clip.

However you have just given Satan a free pass to bring more opportunities to sin into your life. **All Satan needs is for you to commit that first act of sin because he knows that is the first step to addiction.** Next week you will want a folder to hold your personal papers. What about a few of those nice writing tablets for your kids when they return to school and a pack of those compact disk in the back of the supply cabinet.

You know the company buys a load of this stuff every month and it's gone in two weeks so you know other people are taking these supplies so why not you? So you attempt to justify your sinful act of stealing by telling yourself it's ok because everyone else is doing it.

Remember **RATIONAL-LYING** from an earlier section? This is when you lie to yourself in order to clear your conscience. Regardless of what you tell yourself the sin committed remains a sin.

Many lives have been destroyed by sins committed while under the influence of alcohol. The journey down this road to destruction may have started with that first taste of alcohol that someone snuck into a bowl of punch at a high school prom or party. You liked that feeling of being free and loose. Before you knew it, you were the life of the party. Wow, what a feeling!

So you figure, next time, why not have a couple of drinks before the party? That way when the party starts you will be loose as a goose and ready to go! Several years later you are still going, only now you are going to AA. Just one cool sweet wine cooler is all it may take to get some people addicted to alcohol and from there it's a slippery slope to destruction.

Because of our evil desires we are quick to look for ways to justify doing things we want to do even though we know they are the wrong things to do. *For what I do is not the good I want to do; no, the evil I do not want to do-this I keep on doing. Romans 7:19 NIV.*

Sad thing is many parents, often out of ignorance of God's Word, instill in their children the notions that a "little sin" is ok, or "a little white lie" is not really a serious lie. What these parents fail to understand is they are building an access door for sin to enter their children lives. You could make a case that what they are doing is child abuse! We have to train our children in the ways of the Lord.

Controlling the demon of sin acclimation:

Step one: Pray and ask God to give you the discernment to recognize sin before it can entrap you.

Step two: Ask God to give you the discipline to resist any temptations Satan puts before you.

Step Three: Acknowledge you can not win the victory over sin alone. You can only win this battle with God's help.

Step four: When you know you have a weakness for a vice avoid situations that would allow you to be tempted by that sin.

You have to follow a zero tolerance for any vice that tempts you. You cannot have just one drink. You cannot have just one puff. You cannot do just one line. You don't want to be like the frog. What you have to do is just leap away from sin, whatever it is, just leap away and stay away. I know turning away from sin is much harder to do then it is to say. But, that's why you need God in the mix. When God is at the head of your life the Holy Spirit will be in you to guide you away from sin. Remember; *...And God is faithful; he will not let you be tempted beyond what you can bear. But when you are tempted, he will also provide a way out so that you can stand up under it. I Corinthians 10:13.*

Treat every sin no matter how small or innocent it may seem seriously. Don't give Satan even the slightest foothold in your life. If your friends go the way of sin witness to them and depart from them. Don't let yourself be dragged away into sin by "friends".

CONTROLLING FAMILY DEMONS

WHAT A FAMILY SHOULD BE

There are **six basic ingredients** needed to create a properly functioning family; **Love, Trust, Respect, Communication, Compromise and Support.** If any of these ingredients are missing the family will have problems. Now let's take a look at what is going on with modern families.

Our sinful nature and the temptations of a sinful world work to prevent the establishment of ideal families. Our experiences in a sinful world tends to harden our hearts and suppress our emotions until the love we have inside is hard to find and even more difficult to share.

Many non-Christians see any display of love and kindness as signs of weakness/naivety and the mark of an easy prey. To avoid giving the appearance of an easy target we sometimes hide our love to avoid being used or abused. Everyone needs a place where they can unmask, be themselves and feel secure and loved. A properly functioning family is that one place where our love can be freely displayed, appreciated, supported and returned.

What exactly is a family? Modern society harbors many concepts of what a family is but I would like you to consider this one: *A group of persons united by the ties of marriage, blood, or adoption, enabling interaction between members of the household in their respective social roles. God ordained the family as the foundation-*

al institution of human society. Holman Illustrated Bible Dictionary copyright2003.

I like this definition because it includes the notions of being united by marriage, blood or adoption and family members having roles. A man and a woman are united through marriage and their children are united to the family by blood or adoption. The husband, wife and children all have specific roles in the family unit. These roles are delineated many times throughout the Bible. However, they are clearly and succinctly stated in Ephesians 5:22-33 & 6:1-4 and Colossians 3:18-21.

God created man then God made woman to be man's partner and helper. After Adam's sin God required man to work the soil to provide for his family. This established man's role as head of and provider for the family. It also established woman's role as partner and help mate to man and bearer of children. Children's role is to love and obey their parents and contribute to the well being of the family in various ways as they grow into adulthood. After reaching adulthood children are to repeat the cycle by taking a mate and building new families.

Be it a family of man or the family of God (the church) love must reside within the family for it to function properly in accordance with God's purpose. Too often people profess their love for someone or something when they don't really understand what love is. Therefore I direct your attention to the following Bible passages as references to establish the proper understanding of love; *Love is patient, love is kind. It does not envy, it does not boast, it is not proud. It is not rude, it is not self-seeking, it is not easily angered, and it keeps no record of wrongs. Love does not delight in evil but rejoices with the truth. It always protects, always trust, always hopes and always preserves. I Cor. 13:4-7 NIV*

But the fruit of the Spirit is love, joy, peace, patience, kindness, goodness, faithfulness, gentleness and self-control. Against such things there is no law. Those who belong to Christ Jesus have crucified the sinful nature with its passions and desires. Since we live by the Spirit, let us keep in step with the Spirit. Let us not become conceited, provoking and envying each other. Gal. 5:22-26 NIV

Earlier we identified **six key ingredients** of a properly functioning family; **love, respect, trust, communication, compromise and support.** Now let's see how we can define and use these ingredients in building a harmonious family.

Love is the foundation that supports a family structure and without it the family will crumble. Love is the innate tenderness and affection family members feel for each other. It's not something we have to learn, it's in-born. Out of our love we instinctively guard the welfare of our family members. We unselfishly share whatever we have to help family members in need and we support and encourage each other in our pursuits.

Respect is a courtesy we extend to someone we hold in high regard. They are special to us because of the way they properly conduct themselves. Based on pervious experiences in relationships we feel these people will do the right thing in any given situation. Family members that love each other will do the right thing for each other and this fosters respect in the family.

Trust is an assured reliance on the character of someone. In a family this trust is assured based on the love and respect that family members extend to each other on a daily basis over the years. Over the years a family develops confidence in its members and knows they will always acts in ways that guard and support the family. Faith is defined as complete trust. As Christians we have Faith in God. As a family member we should have faith in our family members. However, God will not fail us but sometimes family members may.

Communication is the ability to express oneself both vocally and physically. Communication can be the bind that holds a family together or it can be the sword that cuts a family apart. Kind words and tender touches soothe anger and comforts pain. Encouraging words can put wind to the wings of those weak in faith. Harsh or ill spoken words can crush the spirit, especially in the very young. If family members can not or will not express their negative feelings and concerns, in a constructive fashion, they set the stage for family problems. Problems can only be resolved if they are expressed and dealt with. Otherwise small problems become large festering problems that may explode causing many hurt feelings and possibly serious damage to the family.

Compromise is the ability to reach an agreement through mutual concessions. The key word here is mutual which means giving and receiving in equal amounts; and it also means having the same feelings one for the other. Having established love, respect, trust and communication in the family we have a firm and positive basis from which we can compromise and reach agreements. Once a problem is identified in a family it's imperative that the problem is discussed and worked through until it is resolved by common agreement or compromise.

Support is the act of holding something up, such as the foundation of a building holds up the structure that it is a part of. Family members should hold each other up in difficult times. They must re-enforce and strengthen each other in the face of adversities.

The family's cohesion and unity of support that makes it strong also gives it the strength to survive difficult times and situations. When one member of the family faces a problem the family reacts as though the whole family is

facing the problem and it really is in a properly functioning family.

When I think of family support I think of my uncle Bubba and how he taught me to ride a bicycle when I was
five to seven years old. Uncle Bubba would run along
behind the bike holding it upright as I peddled. Soon after
he let go of the bike I would fall.

But he would not let me give up. I will always remember falling off the bike and him telling me to forget about
it get back on_and let's try again, this time try harder.
Each time I got up and tried harder. Soon I could ride
the bicycle without assistance and I had a great sense
of achievement. If I didn't have family support during my
many failed attempts to ride the bike, my confidence may
have been shaken and it's possible I may have never
learned to ride. My uncle Bubba knew this and that's why
he supported me with his word of encouragement and
his actions. These simple words of support has served
me well, they allowed me to get up, get back on track,
and keep pressing towards my goals in spite of many
failed attempts and difficult times in life. Grandpa taught
his family the important lesson of supporting each other
through words and deeds. Thanks to grandpa, strong
support continues throughout our families even to grandpa's great, great, great grandchildren.

DEMON OF FAMILY RELATIONSHIP CONFLICTS

You must make allowances for each other's faults

and forgive the person who offends you.

Colossians 3:13

Come let us reason together

Isaiah 1:18

There will be conflicts in relationships. The question is what will be the results of these conflicts. *In your anger do not sin. Do not let the sun go down while you are still angry. Eph. 4:26 NIV.* Many years ago in a time far removed from our modern society, life was simple and so were family relationships.

Each family member had a role and everyone did what their role required. Obviously, today's world is much more complex, roles are no longer as clearly defined and relationships are often very stressed because of internal and external pressures.

Societal changes and mass media have greatly influenced attitudes toward family roles. Some fathers no longer want to accept the responsibilities associated with being head of household, they feel the load of providing for a family is too heavy and they should not have to carry this burden alone. Some mothers rightly feel they have the right to a career and an equal or, in some cases, a primary voice in family matters. Some children now feel their desires take precedence over general family welfare.

Many parents feel it is more important, and easier, to be a friend to their children then performing their responsibilities as a parent. Because of the complex, dynamic and sometimes volatile nature of family relations there is potential for much damage when conflicts occur. Considerable time and effort is required to maintain any degree of peace and harmony in a modern household. A key thing to remember, money is not the panacea for all family ills.

I want to put the money issue up front because so many families feel money can heal bad family relations, wrong! God has already provided the key ingredients, freely, for families that will accept Him; **love, trust, respect, communications, compromise and support**. If all members of a family, or any social group, have these things and the fruit of the Spirit is at work in them, they are truly blessed and there are no obstacles they cannot overcome.

Table one show various family relationships; X reflects relations between the husband/father and the family, Y reflects wife/mother relations and Z reflects child relations to family. Box X1 asks what a man would expect to give his wife in his role as a husband. X2 asks what a man would expect to get from his wife in his role as a husband.

Fortunately families generally don't have conflict in all relationships shown in table one concurrently. Typically the conflict would be between husband and wife or parent and child but conflicts can exist between any members of a social group. Let's look at relationship X1, husband giving to wife, and see how the table is used to analyze family relationships.

FAMILY RELATIONSHIP TABLE						
Roles	Wife/Mother		Husband/Father		Child	
	Give	Get	Give	Get	Give	Get
Husband/Father	X1	X2			X3	X4
Wife/Mother			Y1	Y2	Y3	Y4
Child	Z1	Z2	Z3	Z4		

Figure two

Relationship X1, Husband giving to wife: There is a wide range of things that husbands are expected to give their wives and let's call these things **contributions.** However, three of the top ten **contributions** are love, respect and support. This would appear to simplify the relationship but that is not the case.

What is love, respect, and support? Again, there is a wide range of answers to each of these questions. Different cultures, environments and upbringing establish different perceptions of what these things are. Further, they establish varying notions as to how they are displayed.

Some men feel if they work and provide for their family's needs they have adequately met all the needs of family relationship. They feel no need to participate in after-school activities with the kids, movie nights, family dinners, or any other family activities. Some might say this is the old caveman mentality of man hunt and woman do everything else.

Other men work and provide for their families and spend time providing for their families emotional and spiritual needs. These men understand the six key ingredients of a good relationship; **love, Trust, respect, communication, compromise and support** and they also know how to apply these concepts in establishing and maintaining good family relationships. **It is imperative that each family member understand these ingredients are reciprocal in nature; you must give them in order to receive them**.

Next step in analyzing the relationship is to develop an agreed upon definition of the contribution that is made to the relationship. Both parties in the relationship, in this case the husband (giver) and wife (receiver) must agree on the definition. Using the ingredient "LOVE" as a sample contribution this is an example of how a definition may be established;

Husband's definition of love; Work and provide for family, buy flowers for wife on Valentines Day and birthday, and buy Christmas gift.

Wife's definition love; Work and provide for family, buy flowers for wife every week and all holidays, new car for Christmas gift, give wife monthly SPA weekend getaways and help with housework. Be attentive to family's Spiritual and emotion needs

Agreed upon definition love; Work and provide for family, buy flowers for wife on Valentines Day, Mothers Day, and Birthday. Give wife new car every fifth Christmas if possible. Help children with homework three days per week. Help with housework if wife is working outside the house full-time. Be attentive to family's Spiritual and emotion needs

The same method would be used to analyze each family relationship reflected in table one. Clearly all of the six ingredients of a good relationship would be employed in reaching an agreed upon definition of a contribution.

Poor communication is often a key barrier to reaching an agreed upon definition of what a person is expected to contribute. What teenagers perceive as **helping out around the house** and what their parents perceive are often totally different. For example;

Teen's definition of helping out around the house; Take out garbage twice or year if they can remember, clean room when told, cut lawn when told if they can remember. Eat all leftovers promptly.

Parent's definition; Take out garbage on garbage day, keep room clean (by parent's standards), and cut lawn when needed (by parent's standards). Leave some leftovers for rest of family.

Agreed upon definition; Take out garbage on garbage day, clean room weekly, cut lawn at least twice a month during growing season, and leave some leftovers for rest of family. Failure to do these things will result in lost of some or all weekly allowance monies.

Controlling the demon of family relationship conflicts; Earlier we concluded inevitably there will be conflicts in relationships. However, we must learn to control our actions (demons) when conflicts occur. *In your anger do not sin. Do not let the sun go down while you are still angry. Eph. 4:26 NIV.* First we must go to God in prayer and ask Him to give us strength to control our anger and our tongues so we do not sin as we reason together in resolving our conflicts.

Communicating ones' feeling is very important step towards controlling this demon. Suppressed feelings are like an untreated wound, they continue to fester and eventually will do great harm. When my wife and I were spending our first day in our first apartment we agreed to try to settle any disagreements before days' end. At that time I did not have a close walk with God but I had read the above scripture and taken it to heart. We still try to reason together and resolve any conflicts before days' end. I feel that is one of the main reasons for our marriage lasting over 44 years.

To illustrate how critical clear communication can be I will tell you about Bill who was our neighbor in northern California. Our house was one of seven on a cul-de-sac. We started a weekly bible study group rotating meetings between our homes. Initially Bill was not a member of the group but we eventually got the opportunity to invite him to a meeting. After a few meetings Bill began to open up more to the group and told us he had been wrestling with an issue for a very long time and the issue was becoming more pressing in his older years. Bill told us he had not spoken to one of brothers in over twenty years. One year at their annual family reunion Bill overheard a comment by his brother that hurt him very deeply. He elected not to discuss the comment with his brother. Bill decided that since he lived over 1000 miles from his brother he would just keep his distance and avoid going to family reunions if his brother would be there. We prayed with Bill and encouraged him to attempt re-establishing a relationship with his brother.

Bill went to his family reunion that summer and talked to his brother. They discovered the whole thing was a gross misunderstanding. Bill had simply heard a part of the story and had understood his brothers' comment totally out of context. It was all a mistake but that mistake had built a wall between two brothers for more then twenty years. Good news is Bill and his brother restored their relationship, bad news is Bill died two years later. Had all the key ingredients of good relationships; **love, trust, respect, communication, compromise and support,** been working in Bills family Bill would have taken the time to communicate his feeling to his brother the same day he felt offended and they would not have lost those twenty years of brotherly relationships.

There is no magic trick. It takes time and effort to maintain good family relations. However, the time and effort will be well rewarded with a more loving, harmonious and peaceful family.

DEMON OF NEGATIVE RECEPTION

And whoever welcomes a little child

like this in my name welcomes me

Matthew 18:5 NIV

When I talk of receptions I mean the way a person routinely receives people in general, not the occasional time they may receive someone in other than an accepting way. We all have our bad moments. Although I have included this demon under the family demons section it could fit equally well under social demons.

The expression on our face reflects how we are receiving the presence of someone in our life. It maybe someone we just met for the first time or it could be someone that we have been associated with for a longer period of time. Our facial expression, which generally reflects the true feeling of our heart, often betrays us in our attempts to put on a "false front". How family members, or other social groups, receive each other is very closely linked to how well they have worked out their relationships. We use ways to reflect the three basic types of receptions we express to others: **accepting, apathy or rejecting.**

Accepting: An accepting reception is the panacea for so many ills. It can calm a frightened child, reassure a doubtful spouse and uplift an old friend. We all love to see a smiling face; it brightens our mood and lifts our spirits. When a husband or wife arrives home from a hard day of work it's uplifting and comforting to be greeted with a smile from family members. An accepting reception tells a person we care about them and want them to be a part of our life, we are welcoming them into our world. This is so critical to young children when they are exploring life and trying to sort out where they fit, both in life and the family. Imagine a third grader bringing home a failing grade on their school report card. What a relief it would be if mom still has an accepting, smiling face after reading the report card and to know she still loves them in spite of a bad grade. This could be powerful motivation to try harder next school session.

Apathy: To be apathetic towards someone means to totally ignore them as though they did not exist. This refusal to extend an **acknowledgement of significance (AOS)** to a person is one of the most degrading act you can commit against them. You are telling the person not only are you not worthy of my acceptance you are not even worthy of my rejection. I don't love or hate you, you utterly have no significance; you simply do not exist in my world.

Putting prisoners in isolation is based on the premise of denying acknowledgement of significance. The idea is to crush their spirit, their identity and their sense of self-worth. Can you even imagine the devastating and long lasting effect continually denying acknowledgement of significance to a three year old could have on the life of that child? Of course the impact would vary depending on the child but it could significantly distort the development of that child's personality as the child grew into adulthood.

Where so many people are, mostly unknowingly, remiss in their relationships is when they attempt to acknowledge others with things. True acknowledgement of someone requires an investment of your self. You have to invest your time and emotions to show someone they matter to you. Many parents wonder why there is such a gap between them and their children even though they shower them with stuff.

Giving things without any social exchange is of little value in building a relationship. This is just apathy in another form. Giving things can re-enforce a favorable relationship but things alone cannot create a positive relationship. Remember the list of six key ingredients required for a good relationship; **Love, Trust, Respect, Communication, Compromise and Support**. Neither money nor things are on the list.

Rejection: No one wants to enter any environment that makes them feel unwanted or uncomfortable whether it's a social party, country club, family reunion or simply returning home from work or school. We want to feel comfortably accepted in our surrounding, knowing and feeling we belong wherever we are. You may think rejection would be the worst type of reception but it is not. Rejection is not the desired reception however; it is an acknowledgement of significance. In short, any attention is better then no attention. Children, like adults, need that acknowledgement of significance it's like a validation of their existence. Young children that do bad things such as going into the cookie jar or writing on the wall maybe just trying to get attention, even if that attention comes in the form of a rejection of what they are doing

How parents receive their children are the most critical receptions in our society. Children develop most of what will be their adult personalities from birth to approximately age ten. How they are received by others, and especially their parents, during these formative years will greatly influence how they will function as they develop into adults and in adulthood. Therefore people that exercised their right to become parents must also accept the associated responsibility of loving and accepting their children regardless if they are by birth, adoption or step-children. Welcome your children with an accepting reception, and then work out troubling issues through **love, trust, respect, communications compromise and support.**

Let me tell you a little story about two working men. Each man had a wheelbarrow he took to work each day. One man collected every bad thing that happened to him during the day in his wheelbarrow; each insult, fit of anger, jealousy, grudges, etc. At the end of each day he struggled to push the loaded wheelbarrow home where he would dump it in the family room. His anger, frustrations and bitterness presented a hostile and rejecting reception to his family. The other man immediately removes any negative things that were put in his wheelbarrow and at days end he would wash his wheelbarrow clean. Therefore, at the end of the day he had nothing negative to carry home and he received his family with a warm and accepting reception. If you want to have good relations at home don't bring home a wheelbarrow full of negative garbage everyday and dump it on your family and friends.

Controlling demon of Reception: First step in controlling this demon is to learn how to accept and love people more and let God do the judging. When we routinely receive people in a negative way it's because we have judged or prejudged them based on some criteria. That criterion maybe based on facts or opinion but either way it has established a negative attitude towards that person in our heart. True, sometimes people do awful things making it nearly impossible for us to welcome them with a warm reception. However, we must grow in our walk with Christ to a point where we can **love the sinner but hate the sin he commits**. *But God demonstrated his own love for us in this: While we were still sinners, Christ died for us. Rm. 5:8 NIV.*

The first sinner we must learn to love is our self. God's second great command is; *Love your neighbor as yourself. MT. 22:39. NIV.* If we don't love our self, how can we love our neighbor? If a person is happy with whom they are, they are far more likely to receive others in a positive way. Because so many people are so heavily under the influence of the self-hate demon they can't even begin to love anyone else. **Do you love your self?** If you cannot answer this question with absolute affirmation, this is where you need to begin.

Practice thinking positive thoughts about yourself and make a list of the ten best qualities you have.

Make a similar list for each member of your household then focus your thoughts on these positive attributes of your family members.

Do the same for friends and co-workers. The idea is to train yourself to see good in people instead of seeing just negative things in people.

When you feel you have a good list for your family members you may want to share it with them and compare your list with what they feel are their good qualities.

THREE BASIC TYPES OF RECEPTIONS

ACCEPTING

APATHY

REJECTING

Figure three

DEMON OF "NEVER SAY I LOVE YOU"

Love is patient, love is kind, it does not envy, it does not boast, it is not proud. It is not rude, it is not self-seeking, it is not easily angered, and it keeps no record of wrongs. Love does not delight in evil but rejoices with the truth. It always protects, always trust, always hopes, and always perseveres. Love never fails. I Co. 13:4-8.

This bible passage is the Christian standard for a definition of what it means to love someone. Our verbal expression of love should embody all the characteristics expressed in this passage. If we love someone we will be patient with them; if we love someone we will be kind to them and we will not treat them rudely. We express and affirm our love with words and we show and confirm our love through our actions. However, actions alone will not meet the requirement for verbal affirmation.

"I love you too." Four little words, very similar to three little words; "I love you." But the two can be miles apart in meaning. When a person says "I love you too" that person is responding to a statement of love that someone has made to them. If their response is given freely and sincerely all is well. However, if the reply only comes after much delay or even some goading then it's hard to accept the words as being meaningful or truthful. Verbal expressions of one's love for another should be given freely, spontaneously, joyfully and without hesitation or reservation. It is something a person wants to do for someone they truly love, give them a verbal affirmation of their love.

Our oldest daughter rarely tells us she loves us. When we tell her I love you she replies, "Me too". Our two younger children always reply, "I love you too." Seldom will they tell us they love us without us having told them first. We know they love us but we do miss them not being the first to express their love. This, no doubt, is a case of reaping what you sow. I did not verbally express my love to our children when they were young, same as my parents did not express their love to me. I sincerely hope our children will break this pattern by expressing their love to their children.

Many words have been written attempting to explain the various reasons why some people have great difficulty in expressing their love for someone. I know many couples that have been married for many years and love each other dearly but still find it awkward to say "I love you" to each other. Yet, there are very few wives that do not feel warm and fuzzy all over when their husband tells them those three magic words; "I love you." Some husbands buy expensive gifts for their wives when what the wife really wants is for him to simply and sincerely say "I love you". Gifts, things or sex cannot be substitutes for a sincere verbal expression of love. For some husbands those three little words stick in their mouths like a big wad of cheap peanut butter and they just can't seem to get them out.

The saddest and cruelest denial of a verbal expression of love is when it involves young children. From birth to approximately age ten are the most formative years in a child's life. What we do and say as parents and adult figures in their young lives can have lasting impacts. A child never hearing the words "I love you" may never feel loved. They may find it difficult to express their love in adulthood and they may find it hard to understand and accept the concepts of love in relationships.

By verbally expressing our love to our children and confirming our love through our actions, we will build trust, security, stability and a sense of well being into their lives. As parents it's our responsibility to provide this to our children. Again, to do less would be akin to child abuse.

Controlling the "Never say I love you" Demon: Examine yourself and see if this demon is at work in you. If it is you can control this demon by being proactive. Talk to your spouse or significant other and see how they feel about the subject of verbally expressing love to each other and your children. If you find it uncomfortable to verbally express your love to each other or a family member you need to ask yourselves why you feel this way. There may be some issues or conflicts d that family members need to resolve. Have an open discussion and work it through. No one wants your expression of love to be a big dramatic scene or production, just a simple "I love you" will suffice. You can rest assured that ever family member would welcome an occasional sincere verbal expression of love. How they initially react to your expression of love will vary depending on family culture. However, if your expressions are sincere and they are confirmed by your actions you will enhance your family's relationships.

DEMON OF JEALOUSY

A relax attitude lengthens life; jealousy rots it away.

Proverbs 14:30 NLT.

This demon can attack a family in several ways. However the most common forms of jealousy are spousal jealousy and parity jealousy. Whenever one or both of these jealousy demons are present in a family you can be sure one or more of the key ingredients of good relationships are missing and trust is usually among the missing. Two conditions creates a feeling of jealousy; when a person feels someone is attempting to win the affection of someone they value/cherish and when a person feels someone has unjustly gained some type advantage over them.

Spousal jealousy: Newly married couples sometimes find it difficult to trust each other. The most common reason for this lack of trust is simply they don't know each other very well. They may have dated for a long time but that's not the same as marriage. They have committed themselves to a relationship for the rest of their lives and there is no insurance policy to cover the relationship. What happens if their spouse proves to be unfaithful? How can one know for certain their spouse is faithful? They can't know it for certain. There is no way a spouse can be 100% positive their mate is faithful. No amount of spying, sneaking around, checking up, or private investigators can provide the desired proof of fidelity. The only thing that can be proven is infidelity, in the form of adultery. So they need to be very careful what they are seeking to discover, it may not be what they really want to know. People in relationships need to take these words to heart; **you cannot prove a person is faithful you can only prove they are not**.

A marriage has to work on faith which is built on trust which is built over time. If a person gets angry and goes into a rage every time someone looks admiringly at their spouse they have no faith in their marriage. Unless that person change his/her ways their marriage will be a troubled and unhappy one or it will come to an early end. Constantly accusing a person of something is like prophesizing, and we know that prophesies often fullfill themselves. Sometimes a person's accusations can drive their mate into the arms of another. Many times a jealousy person is judging their spouse by their own actions. **Why do you look at the speck of sawdust in your brother's eye and pay no attention to the plank in your own eye? Matthew 7:3 NIV.** A jealousy spouse should ask his or her self these three questions;

1. Am I jealousy of my spouse without any factual proof of infidelity?

2. Am I jealousy of my spouse because I am tempted to be unfaithful?

3. Am I jealousy of my spouse because I am being unfaithful?

If the answer to any of these questions is yes, you need to examine the person looking at you in the mirror. You have to sort out why you are indulging in these type behaviors and refrain from doing them. You may need professional help in sorting these issues out. Repent from these sinful actions; ask God to forgive your trespasses and pray for strength to resist the demons of deceit and infidelity. If a couple's relationship and actions are honest and faithful there will be less cause for jealousy.

Parity jealousy: Comparisons are what sets this type jealousy into motion. One spouse begins to compare his/her self to the other. Who has the largest income, who contributes more to maintaining the home, who holds the highest academic degree, who has the most prestigious job, etc, etc? All of these questions can become issues of contention and serve to push a couple apart.

When one spouse has a significantly higher level income, education, job, or social station in life, comparisons are inevitable. What happens after the comparisons is critical. Once a couple recognizes a disparity in their relationship there are generally three things that can happen: They can accept the situation as a "non-issue" and continue in their relationship focusing on the positives. They may encourage their spouse in working to close the disparity gap, which can be a risky action that may backfire causing a lot of conflicts. Or they may use the disparity as leverage in dominating over their spouse. This is where the daily demons thrive, in dissension. The spouse with the higher level income may use this to dominate over the lower level income spouse or the lower level income spouse may use it to "guilt trip" and dominate their higher level income spouse.

We need to remember, most people continue to grow mentally, spiritually and emotional. Problem is people grow at different rates. Some people are eager to grow, they read everything, they pursue higher education and training, they study, they work hard at their jobs to advance their careers and they are highly motivated. At the other end of the spectrum we have those who have reached a comfortable level of growth and are content to remain where they are. When these two opposites enter into a relationship there are great opportunities for conflict and jealousy. Let's take a look at this story of some friends of ours:

Ronnie, Barbara and their two children were our neighbors many years ago. Ronnie earned a decent living and provided for his family. Barbara took care of the house and children. They were a solid loving family with good relations in the community. When the children were old enough to attend school Barbara decided to return to college and complete work on her master's degree. Barbara quickly earned promotions on her new job and her income greatly exceeded Ronnie's. Trouble began when Barbara wanted Ronnie to help with house work and taking the children to various school related activities. Ronnie refused to do "woman's work". Barbara's position was she was doing "man's work" by providing more money and security for the family then the man of the house. Ronnie's position was; he earned a comfortable living for his family, they were doing just fine when Barbara was staying home taking care of the house and children. It was Barbara's idea to become a career woman and he was not going to do "woman's work". Family relations began to digress very rapidly with Ronnie becoming very jealous of some of Barbara's male co-workers and the new car she purchased. Each one was trying to win the children over to their side of the argument. It just became a very ugly family environment and relationships were awful.

What Ronnie and Barbara had forgotten was a family is not about individuals, it's about the family as a whole. Each member should have been invited to participate in

Barbara's decision to return to college. Any objections and or concerns should have been resolved at that point. Each member should give whatever they can to support the family and the collective family lends its support to each member. When Barbara decided to step out of her role as wife and mother to enter the workforce the family, including her husband Ronnie, should have helped her with family chores. Ronnie must remember his self imposed "house work exempt status" when he was the bread winner of the family. Why shouldn't Barbara have some consideration now that she is making the big bucks? **The name of the game is love, trust, respect, communications compromise and support.** Family members must work together to build a stronger family.

Controlling the demon of jealousy: Communicate, communicate and communicate. People must, calmly and rationally, communicate with each other freely expressing their feelings about things that are a concern. If a spouse feels their love one is giving too much attention to someone else it is imperative they discuss the issue immediately. Holding in one's feeling of jealousy is like sitting on a ticking bomb, it's going to go off and it will make a big mess. And sometimes the mess can't be cleaned up. Talking about the situation removes the fuse from the bomb and allows time to safely dismantle and resolve the issue.

The same applies when one spouse has some advantage over the other; better income, advance degrees, etc. This advantage should not be viewed as a negative thing it should be viewed as a blessing from God to be used to help the family as a whole. Family members should love each other enough to want to share their blessing with each other. Of course family members should not take advantage of a member with a large income. Where there is love jealousy can not prevail. Just as the body is made up of many parts so are the family and all family members should see themselves as all being equal with different roles all working together for the common good of the family.

DEMON OF "I DON'T WANT TO BE A PARENT"

Teach your children the right path and when

they are older they will remain upon it.

Proverbs 22:6 NLT

For the Lord corrects those he loves, just as a

father corrects a child in whom he delights.

Proverbs 3:11-12 NLT

I am starting this section with a story about my pre teen to teenage years. I will use this story to illustrate how my parents provided me with a very precious gift over the course of these developmental years. I focus on this gift and make it the centerpiece of this section because so many parents today fail to give it to their children.

The gift is the **opportunity** to develop a sense of self-worth, self-esteem, self-confidence, self-reliance and independence through achievements. Simply put, my parents gave me the opportunity to develop and grow up by doing things for myself. They taught me the relationship between work and rewards. They provided for my needs very well but if I wanted something extra I had to work to get it. Countless are the times I have thanked them for this gift as it has served and continue to serve me so very well for so very long.

Between ages eight and eleven I did weekly chores and earned a fifty cents allowance each week. I got my first paper route at the age of twelve. This income gave me a great sense of independence in knowing I now had the power to select and buy the types of clothing I wanted to wear to school. When I was a teenager it took me over two years and many hours of working part-time jobs to earn $300 to purchase my first car. What a thrill! I felt like I could do anything! That was my first experience knowing the feeling of significant achievement. My self-esteem, pride and sense of self-worth were all off the charts.

A few of my friends had access to old family cars that they could use on weekends but they were denied the joyous feelings of ownership and independence that was mine. That only comes when you have earned something as I did. When people asked "Where did you get that car?" I found deep satisfaction in replying "I bought it with my own money". I'm much more humble today but still hang on to my independence.

"Oh what fun it is to be a friend, humbug to being a parent." This mantra is acted out many times everyday by parents trying to cope with teenagers, and sometimes pre-teens, over whom they have little or no influence. Generally, the source of the problem in these situations is the parent's inability to grasp their roles in parent child relationship. What they don't comprehend is that in a proper relationship the parents develop the child. The child DOES NOT develop the parents.

Imagine a jar of clear water totally void of color, just clear clean water. Now imagine you have several small bottles of food coloring and you begin to add a little of each color to the jar of clear water. First you may add a little red color, then some blue, then green. Each time you add a new color the jar takes on a different shade. At some point the water in the jar will assume a fixed shade and adding more colors will have little or no impact.

If the proper colors are added the fixed shade will be a beautiful color. If the wrong colors are added the fixed shade will be an ugly color. Once the color is fixed there is very little you can do to change it. You are stuck with what you created.

The mind of a newborn child is like the clear water in the jar, waiting for the colors to be added. That is the responsibility of parents, adding the "colors" to the minds of their children. Some "colors" that may be added are, LOVE, INTEGRITY, COMPASSION, SELF-RELIANCE, RESPECT AND MERCY, to name a few. Parenthood and associated responsibilities are not optional, when you exercised your right to create the child; you are assessed the responsibilities of parenthood. What has to be determined is what kind of parents you will be. My parents colored me well with large measures of self-reliance, integrity and love.

The Bible is very clear, Pr 22:6 *Train a child in the way he should go, and when he is old he will not turn from it.* Your job is to "color" the mind of your child. This is where the Daily Demons come into play. You see the forces of the world (the Daily Demons) would like very much to assume your job of coloring the minds of your children. The "colors" the world will add to your children minds are; greed, hate, lust, envy, murder, rape, addictions, and prejudice just to name a few. Obviously, how your children's minds are colored will greatly determine their future and ultimately the future of the world.

You will have to make difficult choices; will one parent stay at home and develop the children or will both parents pursue a career so the parents can give the children "a better life?" Will you establish and enforce rules of conduct for your children (*Pr 19:18, discipline your son, for in that there is hope; do not be a willing party to his death*) or forsake your responsibilities and become a "friend" to your children?   The Daily Demons will always tempt you to take the easy way out by becoming a friend rather than a parent to your child. By abandoning your responsibilities you leave the task of developing your children to the world.

High cost of living often demands two incomes for a family to maintain a medium standard of living, that's a fact of our modern society. But if we do not make the decisions and sacrifices required to allow us to full fill our responsibilities of developing the minds of our children neither they or society in general will have a "better life". Our future is our children.

People with ugly shaded minds fill our prisons and undermine the tenets of a civilized society. The best way to be a real friend to our children is to accept our respon-sibilities as stated in Pr 22:15; *Folly is bound up in the heart of a child, but the rod of discipline will drive it far from him.* Become real parents that will always love their children first and discipline, not abuse, when necessary. That will be the most valuable gift any parent will ever give their child, the gift of a balanced and properly devel-oped mind. A mind that seeks the truth and is not guided by every new theory, fad or opinion that pops up.

Large boats leave the shores and travel the oceans. As long as the waters are calm and they are headed in the right direction there is no problem. However, when the winds begin to blow and the waters become rough, the boat began to toss to and fro and side to side. It becomes difficult to stay upright. Maintaining a desired heading is all but impossible. The only thing that allows the boat to steer itself in the right direction, towards the safety of calm waters, is its rudder. Without a rudder the boat would be overcome by the rough waters and become lost at sea.

This is why in the early years the boat builders always built a strong rudder and attach it solidly to the boat. The builders took various hardwood planks and joined them together to form a strong rudder. They may have used a combination of Oak, Hickory, Walnut, Cherry and other hardwoods to build the rudder.

It is the Parents responsibility to follow the same approach when "building" their children. They must be sure they solidly attach a strong rudder to their children before sending them out into the high seas of life. .When building the rudder the parents should use planks of Truth, Integrity, Respect, Self-reliance, Responsibility, Good Values, Honesty and other, proven hardwoods. This way the child will be able to successfully navigate the turbulent waters of life. The beautiful thing is when the children become adults they have models to use in building rudders for their children.

Building a proper rudder and properly coloring a young mind are parent's jobs they should not and cannot be done by your government, a friend, or your children's peers. Nor can they be done by parents that will not perform their responsibilities to their children as their parents.

Controlling the "I don't want to be a parent" demon: Parenting is becoming a lost art form and many younger couples struggle with the concept. If you do not understand what a proper parent child relationship is seek counsel from elderly family members, church ministers or other professionals.

Love your children. Even in the most difficult times, always remember they are your flesh and blood. You may hate some of the things they do, but always love the child.

Respect your child and demand respect from them. This is the foundation on which a proper parent child relationship should be built. Always remember, you have to give respect to get respect.

Communicate with your children; really listen to them when they talk. If necessary set aside a time each day to talk with your children so you can know what's going on in each other's life. Communications is the bridge that keeps families connected.

Clearly communicate to your children by your words and actions that you are the parent(s) in the family and that you have responsibilities and authorities they do not have.

Build a trusting relationship with your children. This may prove difficult in cases. The trust must be mutual, you trust them and they must be able to trust you.

Explain to your children that you will always love them even when you do not agree with them or approve of things they have done or want to do.

Also explain to them you will always fill your obligations as a parent even if it means you will not be able to be a friend in a given situation.

Clearly explain to your children that every decision you make and every action you take regarding them is for their benefit. Your actions must backup your words or trust will be out the window in a heart beat.

CONTROLLING SOCIAL DEMONS

HATRED KILLED THE INNOCENT

Figure four

DEMON OF HATE

Acts of the sinful nature are; sexual

immorality, hate...discord and fits of rage.

Galatians 5:19-20 NIV

What is hate? Webster's dictionary tells us it means to harbor; **intense hostility and aversion** towards someone or something. When we dislike someone to the degree that we want to avoid them and harbor hostile feeling towards them, we have hatred in our heart. As a Christian, this is very bad position to be in because; *if we don't love our neighbor who we have seen how can we love God who we have not seen? I John4:20 NLT.* If you have hatred in your heart towards someone there is no room for love.

Why do we hate? Because as all sinful acts, hatred is a result of our evil desires. There are many reasons why one person could hate another with prejudice, envy and jealousy being among the top ten reasons.

Sad thing about hating is it is such a negative, needless and unproductive behavior. Three basic things we need to remember about living a Christian life;

    a. God told us to love our neighbor not with a judgmental love but an unconditional love.

    b. We should give God thanks and praise him for our

blessings and not envy others because of bless-ings God be stores upon them.

c. God works in relationships, just as he works in all things. Therefore we should not be jealous of any one. Therefore, couples, neighbors and friends should spend their time building better relation-ships not on jealousy. If we understand, accept and practice these three notions there would be no room or need for hate in our lives.

Jim who is chief of a six member team drives a five year old Ford. Bill, a junior team member buys a new BMW. The other team members congratulate Bill on his new car. However, Jim begins to burn with jealousy. After all Jim is the boss, he earns a much larger salary, and Bill still has kids in high school and college. It was an affront to Jim's pride that this junior team member could afford to drive such an expensive car and he could not. Jim's jealousy caused him to grow hatred towards Bill. Although Bill was a highly productive team member Jim became relentless in his efforts to undermine everything Bill did. Jim even began to suspect Bill was involved in some illicit activity to pay for his BMW. Eventually Bill be-came frustrated with the treatment he was getting from Jim and transferred to another team. Production at Jim's team dropped sharply when Bill left and Jim was fired. What Jim did not know, and did not ask, was Bill inher-ited a bundle of cash when his uncle, whom he loved much more then the cash he inherited, died.

Two lessons to learn fro this story: Be content with the blessings God gives you and don't envy others for the blessings God gives to them. Secondly, don't judge people because we are not in a position to judge only God is. Just love your neighbor. If they do sinful things, hate these things, but love the sinner and be a witness to them.

Earl was a burly veteran of the Vietnam War having served two years in heavy combat zones. Earl often told his golfing buddy Mitch about his wartime experiences. Earl had several Purple Heart medals for various injuries he received during combat and he was very vivid in expressing his profound hatred, to Mitch and others, of the Vietnamese people responsible for his suffering. Earl resented the fact that Vietnamese were allowed to come to this country and become a part of our society. He felt they were not worthy of being American citizens. Eventually Earl became seriously ill and needed a bone marrow transplant. No match was available and Earl was failing fast. One day Mitch told Earl he knew of a possible donor for the transplant if Earl was willing to accept. Desperate to survive Earl said he was willing to try anything. After many screening test the potential donor was found to be an excellent match and the operation was scheduled. A couple of days after the operation Earl met the donor that saved his life. It was Mitch's brother-in-law Jim Lin a South Vietnamese soldier who suffered massive burn to his body during the war. While on patrol Jim Lin's unit was mistaken for enemy forces and fired upon by an American helicopter killing 17 of the 22 men in his unit.

Earl was shocked and conflicted on several levels to know that this person he had categorized as being less than human had been capable of such an enormous and selfless act of mercy.

Mitch had told Jim Lin about Earl's attitude towards Vietnamese people. However, Jim Lin was more concern about Earl's need than his prejudices. Jim remembered the American medical team that saved his life after the attack on his unit. Jim knew that war is a terrible thing and bad things happen to good people and some times good people do –wrongly - bad things in time of war. It was from this experience that Earl eventually found Christ and learned that we are all one in Christ and in Him there is no hate only love.

Controlling the demon of hate; This demon is similar to prejudice in some ways. They both stir our emotions and form sinful attitudes driven by distorted opinions rather than facts. To control this demon do the following;

a. Get away from the object of your hatred. Give yourself time to cool off and think.

b. Take some time and think about why you harbor this hatred for whatever or who ever.

c. Be honest with yourself in deciding if this hatred is justified. How long has this hatred been inside of you, is it worth the price you are paying? Hauling around a load of hate really is harmful to your health.

d. Ask God to help you dump this load of hate from your wheelbarrow and wash it out.

e. As far as it depends on you, try to make peace with the object of your hatred. If you hate a person that has done you wrong, forgive them. It will be to your great advantage to do this. Just depart from them and go your own way.

f. Just accept God's people as you find them. This is not so easy considering all people are God's even those sinful ones that have not accepted Him. However, through the Holy Sprite that lives in Christians we are able to love and not hate. Your hatred for anyone is a manifestation of the lack of God in your life because if God is in your life you will not hate another.

DEMON OF SINFUL PRIDE

If anyone thinks he is something he is nothing,

he deceives himself. Each one should test his

own actions. Then he can take pride in himself,

without comparing himself to someone else.

Galatians 6:3-4 NIV.

Pride is a word that is often considered a bad or negative word by many Christians. Pride is seen as **a desire
to be God** and is always associated with evil doings,
arrogance, or boasting. However, there is another, positive, application for this word. Take a look at the scripture
above taken from Galatians 6:4; *and then he can take
pride in himself, without comparing himself to someone
else.* When comparing comes into pride sin comes along
with it and then you have sinful pride. Sinful pride is the
root of many evil acts. Greed, jealousy, envy, murder,
lying and stealing are just a few of the negative actions
that are driven by sinful pride. Notice, all of these actions
are self-serving. Sinful pride is all about comparing and
improving one's station in life at the expense of others.
For clarity I will describe two acts of pride, one positive and the other negative. Your son, who has struggled hard with his college studies, brings home all good
grades and you take great pride in his success. This is

positive pride. In the second case everything is the same except you take a copy of your son's grades to work and boasts to a co-worker that your son has better grades then his son. This is now sinful pride because it involves comparing which is judging and judging is sinful.

In the world of aviation, both military and civilian, there is a strict hierarchy of seniority and respect with senior pilots demanding unyielding and unquestioning compliance from junior pilots. For the most part this worked well for a long time but the increasing complexity of modern aircraft and density of air traffic changed things drastically.

There was an occasion when a senior pilot was making an approach at a major airport during a bad storm. During the excitement he neglected to lower the landing gear. The audible warnings failed to activate but the visual warnings did. The junior pilot saw the visual warning and tried to alert the senior pilot of the danger but the senior pilot would not acknowledge the junior pilot. Pride would not let him, the senior pilot, accept the fact that he could have made a mistake and for certain he was not going to let a junior pilot tell him he had made a mistake. Finally ground control detected the problem and ordered the senior pilot to abort his landing. The senior pilot had judged the junior pilot so inferior to himself that his sinful pride would not allow him to accept his warning even in this emergency situation. This incident happened in the mid 1970s and lead to a comprehensive study of cockpit protocol, procedures and safety by a group of military and civilian pilots and behavioral scientist. New procedures, putting safety before seniority, was established as a results of that incident and ensuing studies.

Sinful pride (also called selfish pride) is when one thinks of them self as being more equal to God then someone else. **Their real desire is to be God**. This pride drives evil competition; some people just have to win at what ever they do. It matters little what they are doing or what the cost of winning. It could be winning a board game or winning in the board room. If feelings are hurt, friendships destroyed or lives ruined it's of little or no consequence as long as they win.

Earlier we talked about the human race and a little girl's desire to win it rather than be a member of it; prideful people are in a race of their own to separate them selves from the human race and become God. It's doubtful that anyone consciously starts on a quest to become God. When some people are blessed to have success and as they continue to gain money, stuff, power and social status they develop an insatiable appetite for more.; *whoever loves money never has money enough; whoever loves wealth is never satisfied with his income. This too is meaningless. Ecclesiastes 5:10 NIV.* This is why enough can never be enough for them. They are constantly comparing themselves to others as they acquire more money, power and stuff. True, love of money is the root of all evil but the only reason some people love money is because it buys the things that fuels their sinful pride.

The demon of sinful pride is very insidious. The husband with a wife and two children prays to God for a house in a better neighborhood so his family will be safe and secure. God answers his prayer and continues to bless the family. Years later the husband has stopped praying and spending time with God, he now spend his time flipping houses as he tries to sell their $1,000,000 house in order to buy a $4,000,000 house. The husband no longer views his house as a place to built a loving Christian home, it's just another stepping stone to a higher level of pride. His heart belongs to the things he love, his trophy house, status symbol cars and other stuff. He no longer seeks the joy that comes from serving God; he delights in the temporary happiness received from basting in his sinful pride while comparing his worldly things to those around him. **He no longer has the stuff God blessed him with, the table has turned around, and the stuff has control of him.** The stuff God blessed him with has become the new god that he serves and he is on his way to hell. *You shall have no other god before me Exodus 20:3 NIV*

Controlling sinful pride: The antidote for sinful pride is humility. *He has shown you, O man, what is good. And what does the Lord require of you? To act justly and to love mercy and to walk humbly with your God. Micah 6:8 NIV.*

Out of His tremendous love for the world God gave us the priceless gift of his son, Jesus, while we were still living in sin. God asked very little in return; just three thing. I call these three things God's job description for Christians.

A CHRISTIAN JOB DESCRIPTION

1. **Love God with all your heart mind and soul and keep God first in your life.**
2. **Love your neighbor as yourself**
3. **Spread God's word throughout the world.**

When we perform the task in this job description it will be impossible to indulge in sinful pride because we will humbly honor God our father and always accept him as the head of our life. The job God wants us to do seem simple enough but it really entails turning way from all the sins of the world. If you are busy loving and serving God you will not want to serve the world. This is not to say a person should abandon their friends, jobs or careers; it simply means all parts of your life should be guided by principles that are acceptable to God. If you operate a business conduct you business in a Christian manner that would please God. You can be honest and make a profit because God will bless your business. The same is true for relationships, jobs and careers. If you conduct yourself and perform your work in a fashion that is pleasing to God he will bless you with much success in all you do.

Always keep God first in whatever you do. *Trust in the Lord with all your heart and lean not on your own understanding: in all your ways acknowledge him, and he will make your paths straight. Proverbs 3:5 & 6. NIV.* Recognize God as your Father, the person you go to get answers for all the decisions in your life no matter how large or small the decision may seem. We really never know how far reaching our decisions will be because our knowledge is so limited. That is why we need God to guide our actions because, unlike us, God knows all and sees all.

When you have learned how to do the first task in the Christian job description; love and serve God and he is first in your life, it is easy to master the second task, love your neighbor. When you know how to love God you will know how to love your neighbor without conditions. This is how God loves us; without conditions. You can be certain we will do sinful things God will hate but his love for us will never fail. Like wise, we must love, and not judge, our neighbor even when our neighbor does sinful things we hate.

When we live our lives in a humble and Christian fashion we honor God and put aside sinful pride. The things we say and do become our most powerful witness and testimony to the world for God. This is how we perform the third task of our job description which is spreading God's word. We spread God's word when we control our tempers in heated situations, when we rebuke raging anger with kindness, when we help someone even when we know they cannot return the act of kindness. We spread God's word when we use our time to give words of comfort to someone who is lonely, sick or elderly. It is a most wonderful thing when we spread God's word by teaching and showing children and young people the ways of God and leading them to Christ.

Overcome sinful pride with God's love.

DEMON OF ENVY

And I saw that all labor and all achievement

spring from man's envy of his neighbor, This

to is meaningless, a chasing after the wind.

Ecclesiastes 4:4 NIV

Do not covet your neighbor's

house. Exodus 20:17 NLT.

The first step in preparing to combat any enemy is to know who or what the enemy is. Do you know what envy is? Webster's dictionary defines envy as; *painful or resentful awareness of another's advantages.* The key words here are painful and resentful. Simply being aware of another's advantages is not sinful. It is that demon of comparison that opens the door for envy to enter our soul.

When we have the wisdom to understand and accept God's will in our lives we will never envy another for the blessings God puts in their lives. We will be content in knowing God blesses us with the things that are right for us. A blessing for one could very well be a curse for another.

Two friends work at the same company doing the same job for many years and they are enjoying their jobs and feel well compensated for their work. One of the friends is promoted to a supervisory position and soon envy begins its ugly attack and their relationship begins to deteriorate.

One friend resents the other because he/she is earning a higher salary as a supervisor. What the friend ignores or fails to realize is supervisors take on additional responsibilities in order to earn their higher salaries. Envy driven thought seldom consider facts, it runs on emotions. Life for the friend that did not get promoted has not changed in any tangible way; he is still earning the same comfortable salary without any additional duties or responsibilities and should continue to be content. However, his sinful nature has allowed envy to bring misery into his and compromise a friendship.

I will share a true story with you. In the late 1980s a work associate was having trouble keeping up with his wife's spending habits and they were going deeply into debt. He desperately needed the money associated with a vacant higher paying position although he knew he was not remotely qualified for the position.

His wife used her influence with a company official wife and managed to get her husband the job. Within a few months the pressure to perform in the new position and his inability to do so sent his blood pressure to dangerously high levels. He suffered a major stroke and died 18 months after being promoted into the position. His wife's envy of her friends "superior" stuff cost him his life at an early age.

Seldom if ever will two people be equal in every way. One will almost always have some advantage over the other in some area. This can and should be a good thing because these differences could be a motivating force to push us to improve in our weak areas.

We should neither condemn our self for being weak

in some areas nor envy another for being strong or having the advantage in some areas. We should thank God for the areas he blessed us in and be happy for others when God bless them with his favor.

Most envy is centered on the material stuff of the world. People see others with stuff that they perceive to be superior to theirs and they envy them. What they fail to realize is superior material stuff comes complete with superior liabilities.

A superior $150,000 automobile (we don't call theses cars) will have superior insurance premiums and maintenance cost, an $800,000 house will have superior property taxes, insurance premiums and upkeep/maintenance cost. Most often superior jobs will require superior sacrifices of one's time, self and family. A cost is always attached to every worldly advantage. Some people never realize this and spend their life chasing "superior" stuff.

When you see someone enjoying a perceived advantage ask God is it his will that you should have a similar blessing and if it is ask him to guide your path to this blessing. When you ask God to guide you must be willing to accept his will and His answer. The blessing you desire may not be for you.

Controlling the envy demon: If you feel yourself beginning to envy someone ask yourself these questions;

a. Would the advantage I perceive this person have over me be an advantage for me?

b. Why this person was granted this advantage over me?

c. What could I have done or what should I do to receive the same advantage?

    d. Do I want this advantage, and if so am I willing to make the required effort to earn it?

All true blessings come from God; love, joy, peace, patience, kindness, goodness, faithfulness, gentleness and self-control and in these things there is no envy. Pray and ask God to grant you the wisdom to accept his will in your life and to show you the things that are truly valuable in life. Understand that material things can only be a blessing if they are given by God and they can never take the place of God.

God blesses each of us according to his will for our life. He blesses some of us with a caring heart so they we can comfort those needing mercy and compassion. He blesses others with material things so they may bless those in need by sharing with them.

Think of the world as a chess board and its' 6.5 billion people as chess pieces. God is the chess master and he never makes a wrong move. God places each piece in the right place to do the right thing (His will) at the right time, every time. When you can accept this concept and understand that God blesses people (including you) so they can do His work you will not envy anyone.

DEMON OF JUDGING OTHERS

Accept one another, then, just

as Christ accepted you.

Romans 15:7 NIV.

Do not judge or you to will be judged...Why do you

look at the speck of sawdust in your brother's eye

and pay no attention to the plank in your own eye?

Matthew 7:1-3 NIV.

Looking at Webster's New Dictionary we find that to judge means *to **form an authoritative opinion*** about something or someone. The key word here is **authoritative**. When we are judging a thing it's not very difficult to acquire complete information about what we are judging and be in a position to truly form an authoritative opinion.

However it's not possible for us to acquire complete about a person. We can see what is on the outside but we cannot see the spiritual part that's on the inside. Therefore we can never be in a position to form a truly *authoritative* opinion by which we can judge someone.

There could be any number of reasons why a person's outwards appearance is not up to sociable accepted standards. At one end of the spectrum they could have fallen onto hard times after being down sized from a high paying job and at the other end they could just simply be unmotivated, unwilling, physically or mentally unable to join the work force.

Whatever the case outward appearances doesn't always reflect the goodness or true worth of a person. When we see a person that appears to be on hard times we should understand that except for the grace of God there goes us. It's because of God's grace that we have the ability to have an income and maintain our standard of living.

Many individuals and groups of people judge others based on how they perceive themselves. These people take a phrase that was very popular a few years ago - *what would Jesus do (WWJD)?* – and change it to *what would I do?* They use themselves as the measuring rod or standard to judge others.

Problem is we all have planks in our own eyes so our lives are not good standards to use when judging others. We may not indulge in the sins of the one we are judging but we wallow in several others including the sin of judging. We also fall into the trap of deeming anything we would not do as being wrong or sinful. Many people consider it sinful to consume any alcoholic drink. This is not true. Wine is consumed in many parts of the bible.

However it is sinful to get drunk and lose control of oneself while drinking alcoholic beverages. The sin is in drinking to excess. Some people consider it a sin to play the lottery but there is no biblical foundation for this notion. There is nothing sinful about buying a lottery ticket if you have met all your financial obligations and provided for the welfare of your family. The sinful act is when a person fails to be a good steward over the blessings God has provided such as when they gamble away some of their income and fail to meet their financial obligations and provide for their families.

For example who would be the better steward over God's provisions; a man that earns $1,000 and buys a one dollar lottery ticket each week or the man that earns the same wages and buys himself $500 of fine clothing each week while his family is without adequate food and shelter? Truth is almost anything can be done in a sinful way or to an extent that it becomes sinful. Eating, talking, sleeping, shopping are not sinful acts but they can all be done in a way and to a degree that would make them sinful.

We never know what plans God has for people that come into our lives. We some times establish values, codes of conduct and standards we accept as the benchmark for all others. Anyone not measuring up these benchmarks is judged as lacking without regards to the innate qualities of the individual. Paul, in the book of Acts, is a good example. Before his conversion Saul did terrible things to the followers of Christ.

Christians would not and could not accept Paul as a fellow Christian because he wanted to kill them and destroy everything they represented. Clearly, Paul did not meet the benchmarks of a Christian. Then God called him cleansing his soul, changing his name to Paul and used him to do God's work. No one would have ever judged Paul capable of being a disciple for Christ. We just have no way of knowing what God has in store for anyone because we are all his children and he has a plan for each of us. We must remember that God has HIS plan for our life. It's God's plan that will prevail not ours.

Our plan might be to continue living a life of privileges

but God plan may be to pt us through trials that would reduce us to homeliness so he can humble us then use us
to do His work. So do not judge those that are less fortunate, just love them and help them. After all they may
very well be one of God's projects in progress. We all fall
short and should not judge anyone. Only God is perfect
in all he does and only he can judge his children.

Controlling the demon of judging others; When
we spend our time accepting people and loving them just
as Jesus accepted us, warts and all, we will not indulge
in the sinful act of judging our brother. I know; I really
made that sound far too simple. In reality our sinful nature drives us to look closely at anyone that looks, talks
or acts in a way that is the least bite unusual. If, com-
pared to our perception of normal, they don't measure
up in any way we begin to judge. Most people don't even
think of judging as a sin some even think of it as more
of a duty to be sure that everyone is, you know, normal.
Some people even feel it's the right thing to do; keeping
an eye out for those people that don't fit in with the social
majority, community, or work place. This is a key reason
why judging others is so prevalent, a lot of people feel
obligated to do it.

Some steps in controlling this demon are;

a. Recognize judging it for what it is, sin.

b. Then we must accept all people for what they are
– good or bad - God's creations.

c. Understanding these things we move on to knowing God made no mistakes and all of His creations have a purpose. Therefore we must love
our neighbor –but not the bad things they may do
- and not stand in judgment of him.

d. It is of much greater benefit to spend your efforts
in trying to understand a person than it is to spend

your efforts in judging a person. When possible try talking to the person you feel tempted to judge. Communications often clarifies perceptions and fosters understanding.

e. Try putting your self in the other person's position considering all the circumstances and imagine how you would behave. Would your behavior differ greatly from the person you are tempted to judge?

f. Just remember, when we dare to judge what God has created are we not also judging God? Who would ever be so bold, or foolish, to do such a thing?

Just LOVE your neighbor, let God be the judge.